Amazingly Sew Cute

Turn Scraps into something Sew Amazingly Cute

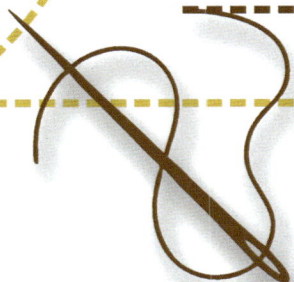

This Book Belongs To

ISBN: 978-1-7333503-0-3 (eBook)
ISBN: 978-1-7333503-1-0 (Paperback)
Library of Congress Control Number: 2019910978

The information in this book is presented in good faith, but no warranty is given nor results guaranteed. Since the author and/or the publisher have no control over choice of materials of procedures, the author and/or the publisher assume no responsibility for any consequences arising from the information, advice or instructions given in this publication.

By purchasing this book, you agree not to share, upload elsewhere, or resell the pattern either as a digital download or printed pattern. You are prohibited from giving or selling any of the patterns in this book to a magazine, blog, or book publisher. You are not allowed modifying the pattern slightly and sell it as your own creation.

Readers are permitted to reproduce any of the items/patterns in this book for their personal use, or for the purposes of selling for charity, free of charge, or home industry and without the prior permission of the author. Any use of the items/patterns for commercial purposes is not permitted without the prior permission of the author. Properly attribute each item (and online listing) that is being made using the patterns in this book is welcome, but not required.

Attention Teachers: The author encourages you to use this book for teaching, subject to the restrictions stated above.

Attention Copy Shops: Please note the following exception - publisher and author give permission to photocopy pattern page for personal use only.

The author and/or publisher are not affiliated with or sponsored by the licensed fabrics used and presented in this book.

Photographs, illustrations, interior and cover designed by Jane J. Wang

Published in 2019 by EZ2Sew Design Studio, a division of EZ Shop & Design Plano, Texas USA
For further inspiration, visit website: www.ezshopdesign.com

Printed in the United States of America

10 9 8 7 6 5 4 3 2 1

Amazingly Sew Cute

Turn Scraps into something Sew Amazingly Cute

Jacine Wang

Dedication

For my grandmother, who is over 100 years old and can still sew by hand beautifully, and to my parents, for raising me to be the best version of myself.

Preface

*I*t never occurred to me that I would have an interest in sewing and write a book about it. The reason I had avoided sewing in the past was because I was always afraid of pricking myself with the needle (even though it still happens) and rarely sewed unless I absolutely needed to.

I never thought I would start my self-taught sewing journey after our family adopted two super cute kittens two years ago; they are my inspiration. In the beginning, I wanted to make a comfortable hammock for them, which required some sewing. I tried to avoid hand-sewing, and ended up ordering a sewing machine, which I wasn't very familiar with. After giving it a try and learning my way around the sewing machine, I grew to love sewing, designing bags, and more. Even though I experienced many challenges as I was learning, I have a lot of fun sewing. Not to mention, our two kitties are always playing and napping around my workspace. I wouldn't have imagined that sewing would bring me so much joy and am unable to go a day without it.

Jacine ♡

05.20.2019

Table of Contents

Essential Tools 1

Fabrics & Interfacing 6

Hardware 11

Basic Stitches 13

Install Sew-In Purse Frame 16

Sewing Curved Seam 27

How to Use the Pattern 30

    How to Use the Pattern 31

    Understand the Pattern 33

    How to Modify the Pattern 36

The Katy - One piece, Oval Shape Frame

    Ava 42

    Brooklyn 54

The Katy - One piece, Round Shape Frame

    Charlotte 60

    Daisy 69

    Evelyn 71

The Katy - Two pieces, Round Shape Frame

    Faith 75

The Katy - Three pieces, Round Shape Frame

    Grace 88

    Hope 98

    Iris 102

The Katy - Four pieces, Round Shape Frame

    Jade 114

    Kaylee 124

The Katy - Four pieces, Oval Shape Frame

    Lauren 128

    Mila 137

The Katy - Five pieces, Round Shape Frame

    Nova 140

    Olivia 150

Acknowledgements

*S*ewing and designing patterns may not be that hard, but writing a book about how to sew is much harder than I imagined. None of this would have been possible without my family's support and encouragement.

To my mom, my sister, Ling-Ling, and my husband, Charles, thank you for supporting and encouraging me to pursue my newfound interest.

To Christine, my daughter, for doing some projects with me when I first started sewing. Thank you for working with me and having fun.

To Johnathan, my son: thank you for taking the time to read my drafts and edit it for me. Editing is not an easy task, but you are so patient with me.

Our family's two kitties, Asti and Celine, you are my inspirations. Beside my kids, you are cute little angels as well. Thank you for accompanying me while I work.

The most important thing is to thank you for purchasing my book, providing amazing feedback and encouraging me to continue to write more!

Even though I am not affiliated with or sponsored by the licensed fabrics, I still want to thank them for creating and designing the beautiful fabrics presented in this book.

Introduction

I love handbags like many women, but I can't find the "perfect" one that meets all my needs. After starting to learn how to sew, I began to design and make my own, combining things that I thought would make the "perfect" purse for me. After sewing many projects, I found that I have lots of scraps left. Most of the time we don't know what to do with those scraps; some of them are too big to throw away but not big enough to make another project.

One day, I found out that I had an old frame coin purse in my closet. I think the frame purse is more retro and classic. I've tried to design and make a few out of curiosity. While designing bags based on the same frame, I was able to create a variety of styles, full of imagination and innovation. I learned from the failures and gradually got better at it. The process of designing, making, and finishing is a lot fun. I fell in love with making these small, adorable, and elegant frame purses.

In this book, I will be sharing my patterns and instructions for making these incredibly cute frame purses. For beginners, it's very easy to learn. For those who don't know how to use a sewing machine, like me before, all these projects can be hand-sewn. I hope you will enjoy the process of making them.

Essential Tools

Craft Shears
A good pair of craft scissors can be used to cut the patterns.

Fabric Cutting Shears
Fabric cutting shears are used for cutting fabric.

Pinking Shears
Pinking shears have blades with serrated edges. They leave a zigzag pattern after cutting. They are useful for trimming off excess material on a curved seam to reduce the bulk.

Rotary Cutters
There are different sizes of rotary cutters: 60mm, 45mm, 28mm and 18mm. The 18mm and 28mm are more helpful for the patterns mentioned in this book because of the size of the pattens you will be cutting and the accuracy required to cut them.

Craft Knife
There are some markings from the patterns that need to be transferred onto the fabric after cutting. The craft knife is useful for this but could also use a marking pen or tailor's chalk instead.

Cutting Mat
The cutting mat is used to protect the table while you cut the fabric and transfer the markings.

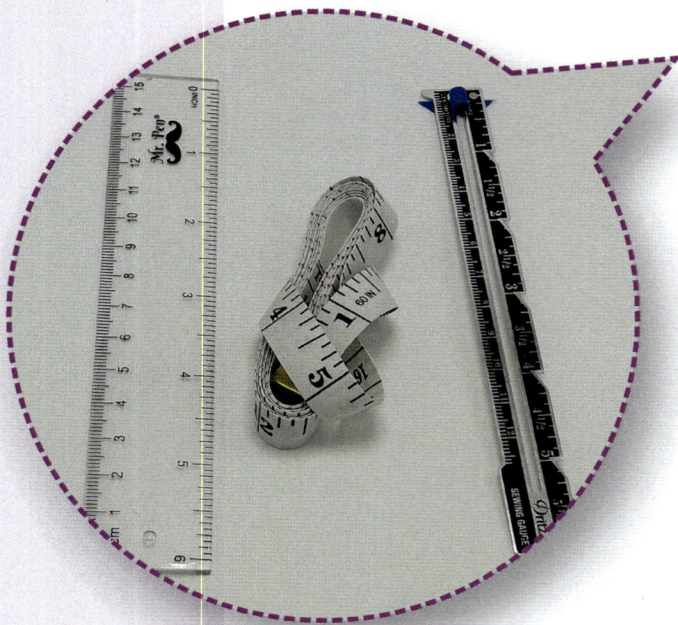

Clear Ruler

A ruler is used for drawing straight lines.

Seam Gauge

The seam gauge is useful for adding seam allowance around the patterns if the pattern doesn't include seam allowance.

Tape Measure

The tape measure for sewing is a flexible ruler used to measure length, width, and height.

Thread Snips

Thread snips, thread nippers, or thread clippers are a must in a sewing kit. They cut threads quickly in tight corners that larger scissors can't reach.

Seam Ripper

The seam ripper is used for removing stitches. You will need this tool if you accidentally forget to leave an opening for turning the purse right side out.

Awl

This tool is optional. If you feel the piece is too small to feed through the presser foot using your fingers, it can act as an assistant to feeding the fabric.

Fabric Marking Pencils
Tailor's Chalk
Erasable Gel Pens

These are used to trace patterns, draw seam allowances, and make markings on the wrong side of the fabric. If you need to make markings on the right side of the fabric, use a heat or water erasable pen.

Sewing Pins

Sewing pins are used to temporarily hold the fabric in place while cutting several layers or sewing.

Clips

If you don't like using pins to hold the fabric in place while sewing, clips will do the same job. I use sewing pins while cutting several layers of fabric and use clips while sewing.

Pin Cushion

A pin cushion is used to store pins or needles.

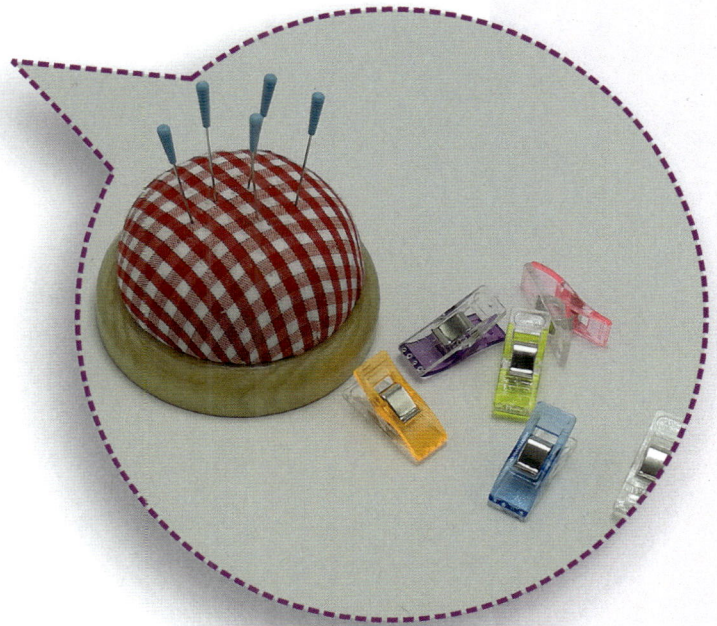

Iron and Ironing Board

The iron is used to press the seam allowance, flatten the fabric and apply the interfacing. It can also shape the finished purse. The ironing board is used to protect the surface under the iron.

Hand Sewing Needles

A lot of the projects included in this book required hand sewing. It is possible to hand-sew entire projects without the sewing machine. Thus, it's very important to have a few good sewing needles.

I would also recommend using a *Thimble* while installing the frame on the purse. This tool is used to push the needle throughout layers of fabric without hurting your fingers.

Sewing Machine

You don't need a fancy or complicated sewing machine. Any sewing machine that can sew a straight line will get the job done.

Fabrics & Interfacing

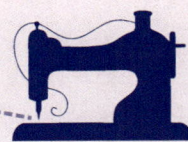

Fabrics

We call them "fabric scraps". That's right! How many of us have some fabric too small for a big project, but too big to throw away? We hope to use them in another project but can't find a place for them.

I have a great idea for you!

In this book, we will grab those so called "scraps" to make something so adorable and useful!! It could become a lovely gift for your friends and family for any occasion.

What type of Fabric can we use?

Any kind of fabric from cotton to medium weight, such as quilting cotton, linen, micro-suede and corduroy could be used. We will try to avoid any fabric that is too thick or too heavy.

There are many kinds of interfacing on the market. In this book, I used quilting cotton as the main and lining fabric. The two types of interfacing that I chose to use are:

For Exterior/Main:

★ If you are using thicker fabric than quilting cotton, such as micro suede or corduroy, you might want to apply **Single Layer** interfacing, _Pellon SF101 Shape-Flex Woven Fusible Cotton_.

★ If you are using quilting cotton, you can apply either **Single Layer**, _Pellon 987F Fusible Fleece_ ONLY, for more softness, or apply **Double Layers**, combining _Pellon 987F Fusible Fleece_ with _Pellon SF101 Shape-Flex Woven Fusible Cotton_, to have more structure and still feel soft.

Interfacing

For Interior/Lining:

★ Apply **Single Layer** interfacing, _Pellon SF101 Shape-Flex Woven Fusible Cotton_, if you choose quilting cotton as your lining fabric. I would not recommend using fabric that is too thick for the lining.

★ If you are using silk, for instance, you might want to leave the fabric as is; you don't have to use any interfacing.

If you would like to have a more structured look, _Pellon SF101 Shape-Flex Woven Fusible Cotton_ is a good choice.

For those who can't find the interfacing mentioned above, you may find any similar types of woven or fleece interfacing as a substitute.

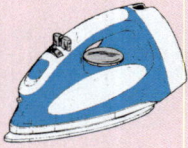

Apply Interfacing

Interfacing:

❶ **Pellon 987F** - Pellon 987F Fusible Fleece

❷ **Pellon SF101** - Pellon SF101 Shape-Flex Woven Fusible Cotton

*A*lways follow the manufacturer's directions for applying any interfacing to the fabric.

*T*est before applying to any main fabric.

Apply Single Layer Interfacing

① Place the fabric wrong side up on the ironing board;

② Place the fusible interfacing (either ❶ or ❷) on top, with the adhesive side (bumpy side) faced down on the wrong side of the fabric;

③ Cover the fabric and interfacing with a press cloth or a heat resistant craft sheet, and press the iron onto it.

④ Make sure the interfacing attached well onto the fabric.

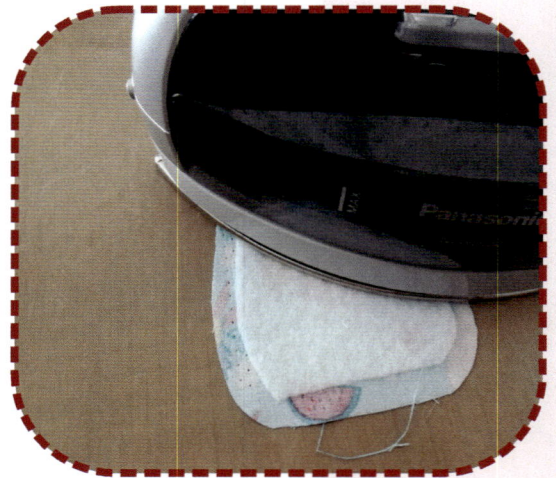

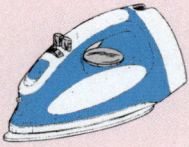

Apply Interfacing

Interfacing:

❶ *Pellon 987F* - Pellon 987F Fusible Fleece
❷ *Pellon SF101* - Pellon SF101 Shape-Flex Woven Fusible Cotton

Apply Double Layers Interfacing

① Place the fabric wrong side up on the ironing board;

② Place the fusible interfacing ❶ on top, with the adhesive side (bumpy side), faced down onto to the wrong side of the fabric; Cover the fabric and interfacing with a press cloth or a heat resistant craft sheet, and press the iron onto it.

③ Place the fusible interfacing ❷ on top of the fusible interfacing ❶ with the adhesive side faced down; Cover the fabric and interfacing with a press cloth or a heat resistant craft sheet, and press the iron onto it.

④ Make sure both layers of interfacing attached well onto the fabric.

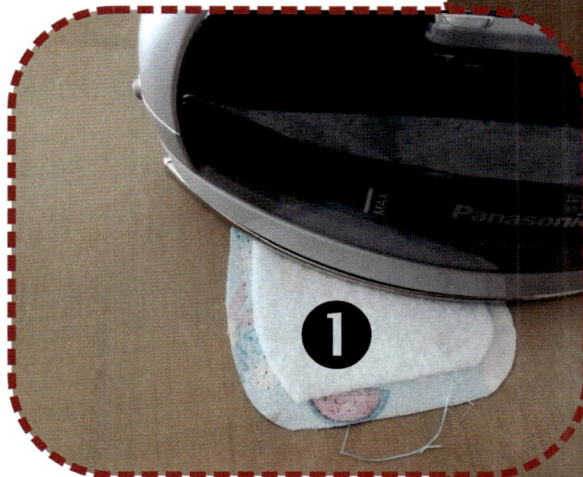

Hardware
Kiss Lock Purse Frame

Round

Round

Round

Round

Oval

3.35" (8.5 cm)

3.35" (8.5 cm)

Kiss Lock Purse Frame plays a leading role in all of the projects mentioned in this book. There are many shapes (rectangular, curved/arch, m-shape), sizes (from mini, small to large) and colors (gold, silver, bronze, black) of purse frames out there and two types of installation methods: sew-in and glue-in. There are many different kinds of lock shapes on top of the frames that you can choose from as well.

In this book, we are going to use the **_Size: 3.35" (8.5 cm)_**, **_Shape: Curved/Arch_** **(Half Round/Oval)**, **_Installation: Sew-in_** style purse frame to finish all the projects. The pattern will indicate which **shape (Round/Oval)** of purse frame is going to be installed after completing the purse piece. **_Do NOT install a frame with the wrong size and shape to the purse,_** otherwise it won't fit or look well. If you don't like the sew-in style frame, you might use glue-in frame as well. But make sure the SIZE and SHAPE match the pattern.

Basic Stitches

Basic Stitches

*S*ince we are going to be installing a sewn-in purse frame to the purse pieces, we need to know some basic hand sewing stitches.

Running Stitch

The running stitch is a basic and very simple stitch that most beginners should know how to do. The running stitch can sew straight and curved lines in hand sewing and embroidery. If you don't want to or don't know how to use a sewing machine, using the running stitch with a small interval between stitches works as well.

Ladder Stitch

No matter what you want to call it, the Blind/Slip/Invisible stitch is very useful for closing gaps and openings after turning the purse right side out.

Gap/opening

Right side of the fabric

wrong side folded seam
wrong side folded seam

❿ ❼ ❻ ❸ ❷

❾ ❽ ❺ ❹ ❶

knot is hidden under the wrong side folded seam

Right side of the fabric

Basic Stitches

Back Stitch

① If you are using sewing machine, please remember to backstitch at the beginning and the end of all seams to secure them.

② If you are hand sewing, this is another useful stitch to sew without using a sewing machine.

③ A simple Back stitch can be used for starting and ending the installation of the purse frame on each side of the purse frame. Please refer to the Chapter "Install Sew-in Purse Frame".

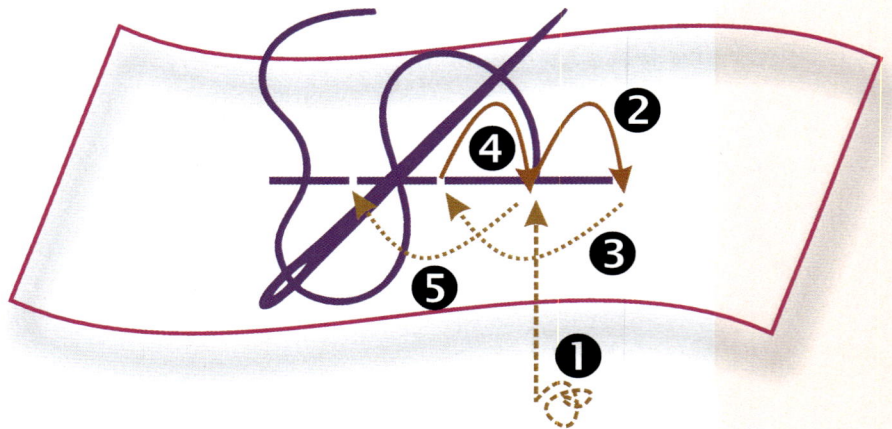

Basting Stitch

The basting stitch is a longer version of a running stitch, sometimes with or without tying a knot at the beginning or end. We are going to use the basting stitch for temporarily holding the frame to the top of the finished purse piece while installing the purse frame onto it. You may use other solutions (using pins or clips) to temporarily hold the purse frame while installing.

Install Sew-in Purse Frame

Keys to Success

Practice

Practice is the first and most important key to success, especially slow practicing. If you would like to have an adorable finished project, SLOW PRACTICE is key.

Patience

The second key to opening the door of success is patience, always paying attention to the small details. Accurately cutting the patterns and fabric, taking time to transfer every marking to the fabric means no rushing! One step at a time.

Passion

The final key to a successful project is passion. No one can force you to do something you don't like unless you have passion to do so. **DO WHAT YOU LOVE AND LOVE WHAT YOU DO.** *And, ENJOY whatever you do, ALWAYS!!* ☺

All the projects in this book are easy to sew; nothing is "sew" difficult. If I were to pick one of the most difficult things about finishing these projects, it would be installing the purse frame onto the finished purse piece. Other than that, it should be fairly easy to follow along.

There isn't any particular way to sew in the purse frame onto the purse piece. You can use the running stitch to sew through twice (once forwards and then again in reverse), or use back stitch.

Here, I would like to share with you how I install the purse frame. Personally, I prefer using the slip stitch. It leaves fewer visible threads inside the purse under the frame, unlike the running stitch or back stitch. You only need to sew through the frame once unlike the running stitch which requires it to be sew through twice on each side.

Since installing the purse frame is a little bit challenging, it wouldn't be an issue if you practiced slowly and patiently. Let's understand how it works before starting to make the purse piece.

DIRECTIONS

Get the Tools Ready

1 *Needle Puller:* Use on finger to grip and pull needles.

2 *Thimble:* Finger protector. Use on finger to push the needle into several layers of fabric.

3 *Thread Nippers/Snips:* For snipping threads.

4 *Screwdriver:* A small flat head screwdriver is used for tucking the purse piece into the frame track.

5 *Needle:* A good strong hand sewing needle is used for sewing the frame and purse piece together.

6 *Pin and Pin Cushion:* Pin is used for temporarily holding the purse piece and frame in place. Pin cushion is used for storing needle and pin.

7 *Threads:* There are many types of threads you can choose from, for instance, Cotton threads, Nylon/Rayon threads, Polyester threads and invisible threads to complete the project.

Color of the threads:

★ *Invisible threads* - It won't leave noticeable threads at the exterior and interior. Some of the invisible threads are very slippery. If you are installing the purse frame for the first time, I would recommend using non-slippery types of threads until you are familiar with how the installation works.

★ *Coordinating threads* - You may coordinate the color of the Main/Exterior or Lining/Interior fabric.

★ *Contrasting threads* - If you would like a more colorful project, any contrasting color or rainbow color will work as well.

DIRECTIONS

Before Installing the Purse Frame

1 Get your completed purse piece and the purse frame ready for the next step.

2 Find the centers of each side (4 sides) and make markings by using fabric pen or pencil on the completed purse piece.

3 Align all 4 centers on both the purse piece and the frame. Tuck the top of the purse piece into the frame track.

4 Use pins to hold them in place. Make adjustment until all 4 sides are aligned into their center positions. Use the Basting stitch to hold both pieces together temporarily, so it won't move around while installing. *Remove the basting stitches after completing installation.*

DIRECTIONS

Where to Start Sewing

*T*here are many ways to install the purse frame. You may start sewing from the center, left or right, depending on your preference and the installing method you choose.

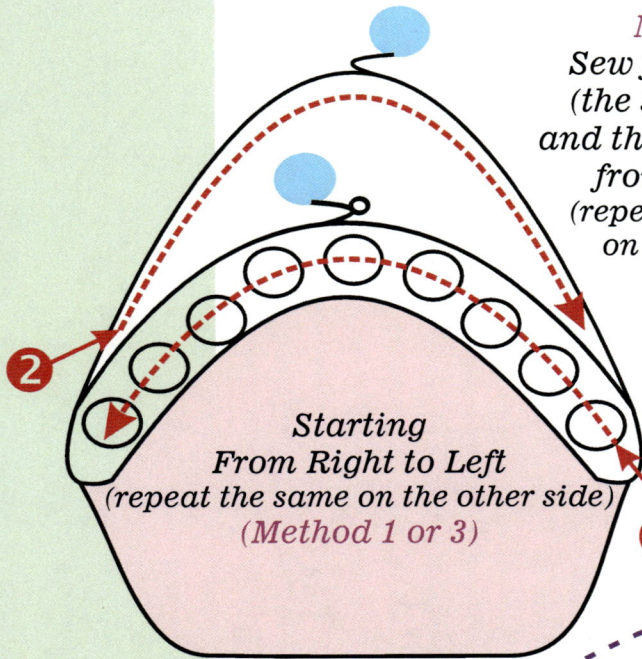

Method 2
Sew from ❶ to ❷
(the same side)
and then in reverse
from ❷ to ❶.
(repeat the same
on the other
side)

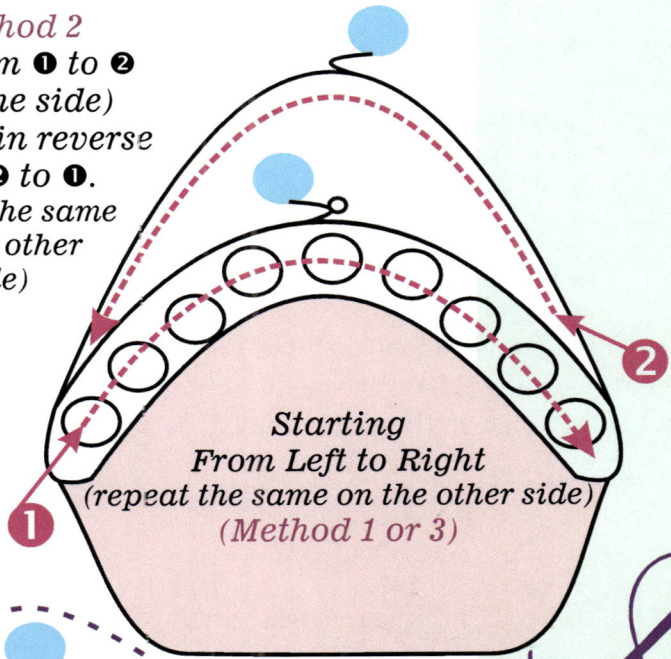

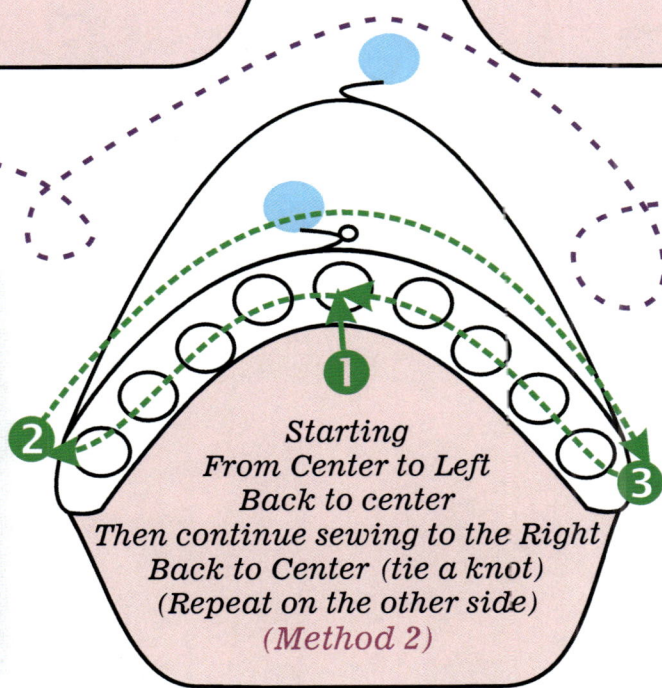

Starting
From Right to Left
(repeat the same on the other side)
(Method 1 or 3)

❷

❷

❶ ❶

Starting
From Left to Right
(repeat the same on the other side)
(Method 1 or 3)

Sewing Method

Method 1
Slip Stitch

Method 2
Running Stitch

Method 3
Back Stitch

❶

❷

❸

Starting
From Center to Left
Back to center
Then continue sewing to the Right
Back to Center (tie a knot)
(Repeat on the other side)
(Method 2)

*I*f you prefer to start from the center on each side of the frame, use Method 1 or 3:

★ Sew from ❶ to ❷, then tie a knot, then from ❶ to ❸, tie a knot.
★ Repeat the same on the other side of the frame.

DIRECTIONS

Method 1 - Slip Stitch

1 Starting from the inside, pull the needle through the 1st hole and pull all the way through.

2 From the outside, push the needle through the 2nd hole.

3 Loop the needle back into the 1st hole again.

4 Push the needle through the 2nd hole again, ending with the thread on the inside.

The steps above are called "Back" stitching, securing the thread. We will do these steps again when we reach the last 2 holes on the same side of the purse frame.

DIRECTIONS

*A*fter step 4, the needle should on the inside of the 2nd hole.

5 Now, place the needle next to the last stitch about 1/16" (1~2mm) away from it, then from the same hole, pull the needle through to the outside.

6 Moving to the next hole, push the needle through to the inside.

From inside the 3rd hole, repeat these 2 steps until reaching the last 2 holes.

*A*fter repeating steps 5 and 6 several times, finally, we reach last two holes.

7 Now, the needle should be on the outside of the 2nd to last hole. Push the needle into the last hole from the outside.

8 We need to secure the thread and do the "Back" stitch, like we did with the first 2 holes. Loop the needle back into the 2nd to last hole again, ending up on the outside.

9 Push the needle back into the last hole, ending up on the inside. Move on to step 10, or repeat steps 8 and 9 one more time.

10 Tie a knot and cut the remaining thread tail.

Repeat steps 1~10 with the other side of the frame. Remove Basting stitches if you used them.

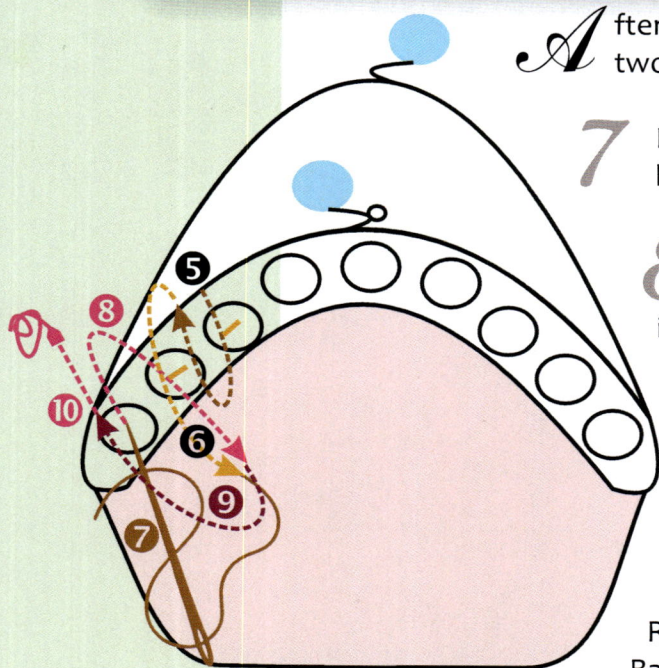

DIRECTIONS

*B*y using **Method 1 - Slip Stitch** to install the frame to the purse piece, the interior will appear like dots under the frame and the exterior will have dashes that connect each hole.

You may use **Method 2 - Running Stitch** or **Method 3 - Back Stitch** to install the frame as well.

By using the Slip Stitch to install the frame, it will leave small dots in the interior and dashes on the exterior.

Type of Thread

★ *Invisible/Nylon threads*

Color of Thread

★ *Invisible*

DIRECTIONS

Method 2 - Running Stitch

*R*unning Stitch can be used for installing the purse frame as well.

1 From the inside, pull the needle through the 1st hole ending on the outside.

2 Moving on to the 2nd hole, push the needle through to the inside.

3 Onto the 3rd hole, pull the needle through ending up outside.

4 To the next hole, push the needle through to the inside.

Repeat steps 3 and 4 until you reach to the last hole on the same side of the purse frame.

5 Travelling in reverse, push the needle into the 2nd to last hole, back into the inside.

6 Continue in reverse, pulling the needle out of the next hole.

Repeat steps 5 and 6 until you reach to the first hole at the beginning on the same side of the purse frame.

7 "Back" stitch at the first 2 holes and tie a knot from inside.

Repeat the same steps above on the other side of the frame. Remove Basting stitches if any were used.

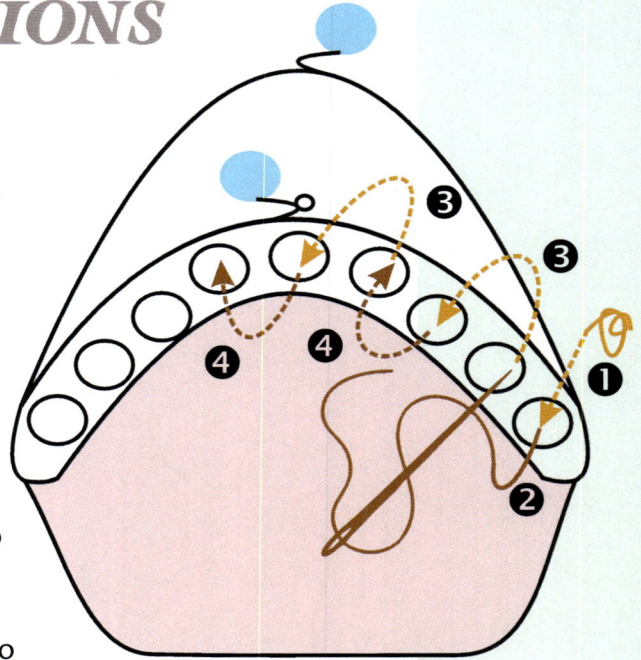

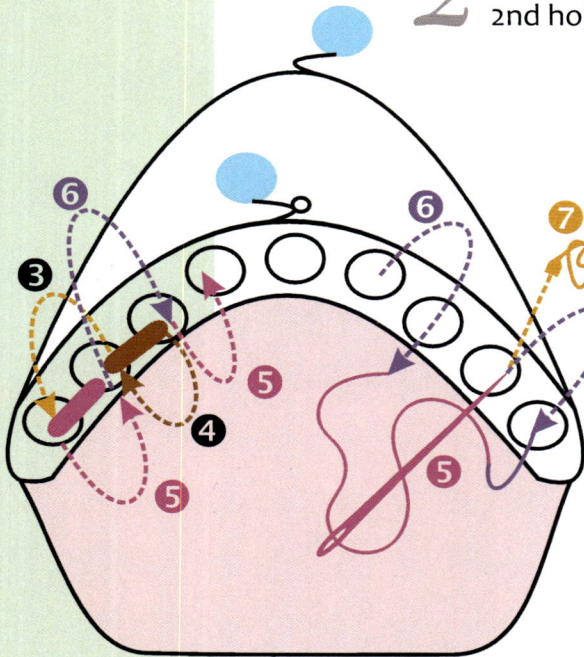

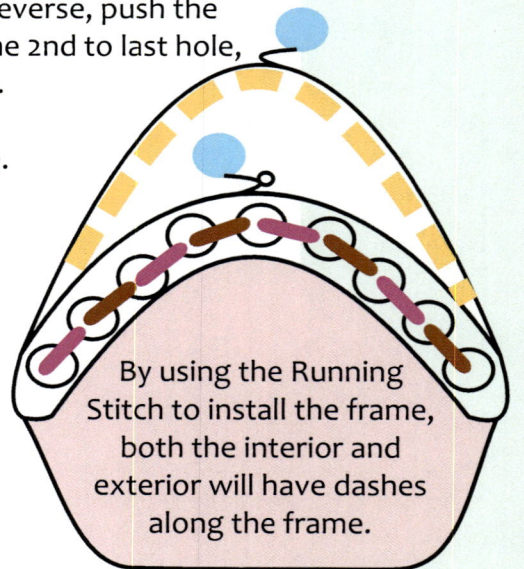

By using the Running Stitch to install the frame, both the interior and exterior will have dashes along the frame.

DIRECTIONS

Method 3 - Back Stitch

*B*ack Stitch can be another way for installing the purse frame as well. This method will leave the most visible threads on the inside, under the frame.

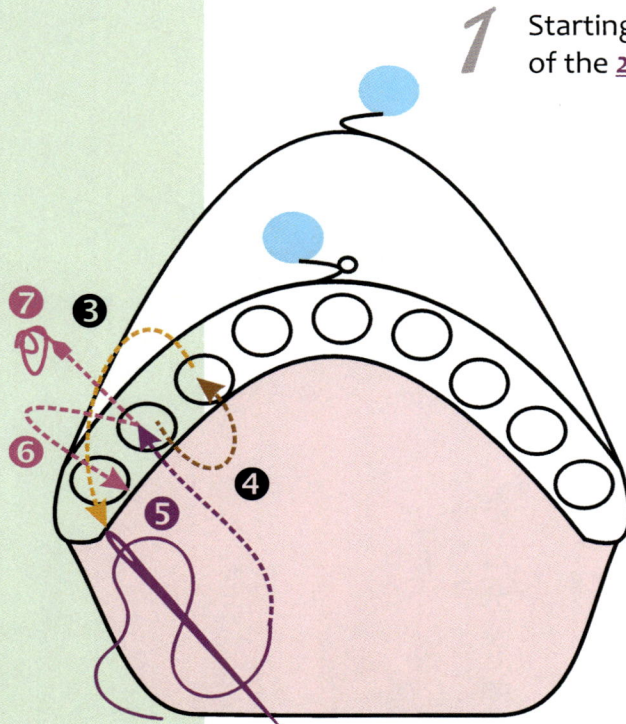

1 Starting the inside of the **2nd** hole, pull the needle out.

2 Back to the 1st hole, push the needle in. Repeat steps 1 and 2 for more security if needed.

3 Moving to the 3rd hole, pull the needle towards the outside.

4 From the previous hole (2nd hole), push the needle to the inside of the frame.

Repeat steps 3 and 4 until you reach to the last hole on the same side.

5 Upon reaching the last hole, the needle should be on the outside. Loop back to the previous hole and push the needle inside.

6 Back to the last hole, pull the needle out.

7 Repeat steps 5 and 6 once more to secure the threads before tying a knot in the 2nd to last hole.

Repeat the same process on the other side of the purse frame. Remove Basting stitches if any were used.

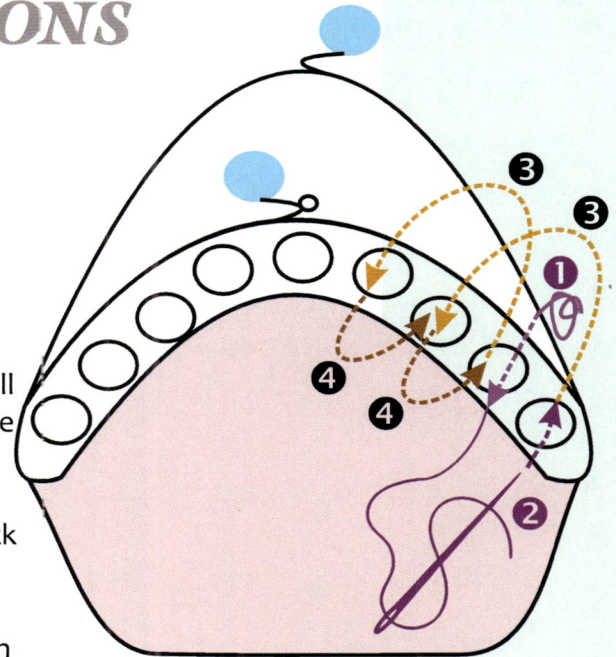

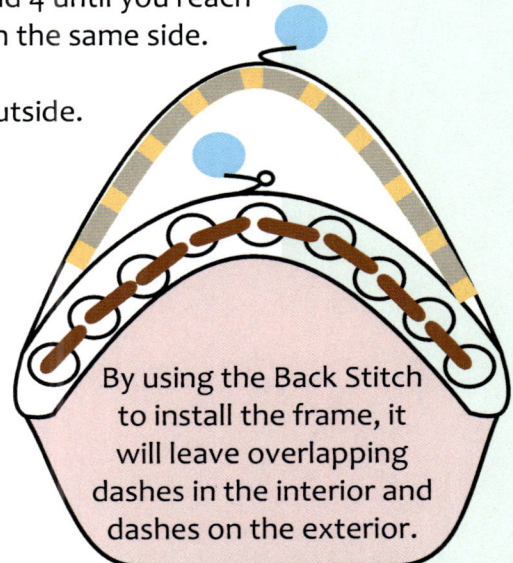

By using the Back Stitch to install the frame, it will leave overlapping dashes in the interior and dashes on the exterior.

Sewing Curved Seam

DIRECTIONS

Sewing the Curved Seams

*S*ome of the patterns mentioned in this book have curved seams, so let's talk about how to make those curved seams, smoothly. There are many wonderful articles and tips on the internet that talk about how to sew curved seams, if you are interested in a more in-depth explanation. I would highly recommend looking into it.

1 **Trace the Pattern.** Trace the pattern by using chalk or erasable pen to the wrong side of both connecting fabrics. This will be the sewing guide line and help you focus on the fabric while sewing, regardless if you are hand sewing or using a sewing machine.

2 **Match the center markings.** Match both fabrics on the centers, then clip or pin in place. Place the piece with the curved seam under the piece with the straight seam, right side facing each other.

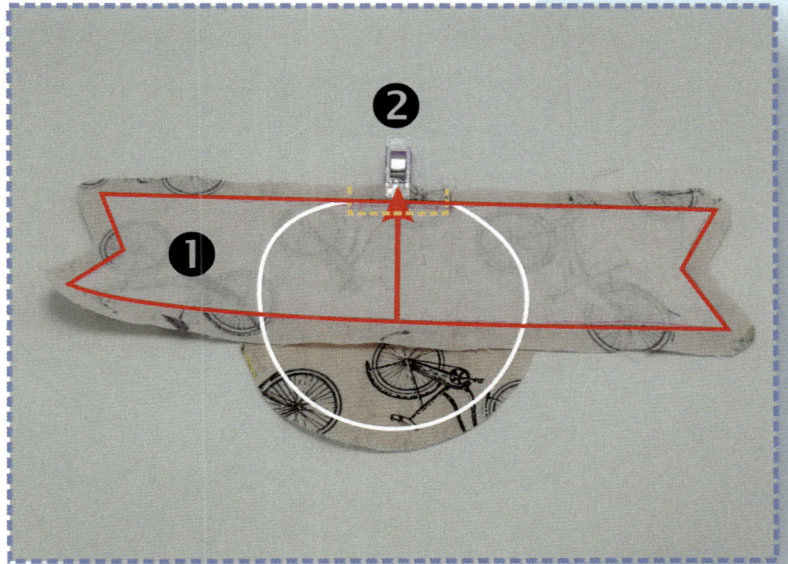

3 **Hold in Place (Optional).** At the center of the straight seam piece, you might want to sew this place first to hold both pieces in place.

4 **Snips in Curves.** Near curved areas where both pieces meet, cut a few slits on the top piece (straight seam piece) so that the fabric will become more flexible to match the bottom fabric with curved seams.

DIRECTIONS

5 *Match the rest of Markings.* Match the side markings on both sides, pin or clip all the way around.

6 *Sew.* Sew all the way around. If you did step 3, sew halfway until you meet the straight seam, and then finish the other half.

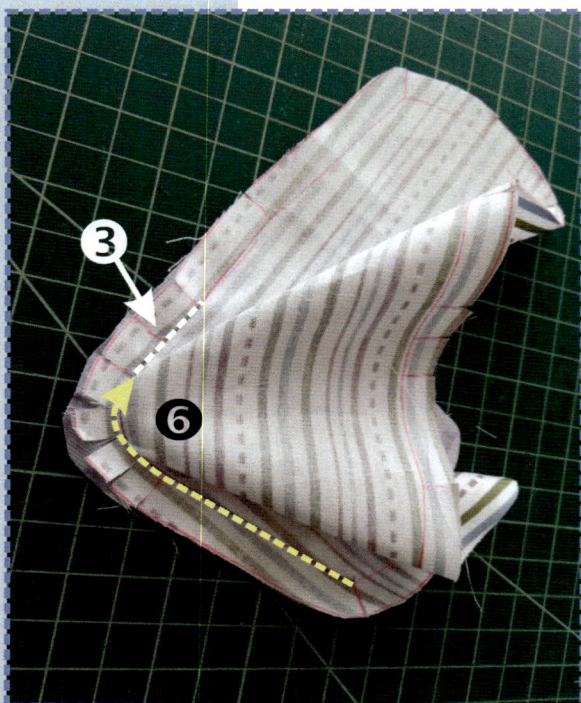

5 *Smooth Out Curve.* Turn your project right side out, smoothing out the edges by pushing out the curved seam with a pointed object such as a knitting needle, a chopstick, or your fingertips. DO NOT use something too sharp, like a knife, otherwise you'll poke through the seam line.

A Few Tips

① *Shorten the Stitch Length.* Sewing around the curves is easier with shorter stitches. Smaller stitches make a curve look less angular.

② *SLOW DOWN, WATCH and PIVOT.* Use the hand wheel to drop the needle down into the fabric, then lift the presser foot and pivot while sewing the curves. ***Do NOT rush, SLOW DOWN.***

③ *Cut Notches or Slits.* Once the piece has been sewn, use pinking shears to trim the fabric within the seam allowance to minimize the bulk. This will be important later on when you turn the piece right side out. Be careful not to cut into your stitches!

④ *Press Well.* Press the seam open with your fingers and then iron it with a little steam to remove bumps and wrinkles.

How to Use the Pattern

DIRECTIONS
How to Use the Pattern

*L*et's get the pattern ready so we can start sewing our projects. *__All the patterns in this book have NO SEAM ALLOWANCE included.__* Before we start to cut the fabric, we need to do some preparations for the pattern.

1 **Print out or Trace the Pattern onto paper.** Trace the pattern by using tracing paper from the pattern page, or print out the pattern from the pattern page (check the Printing Instructions below). Make 2 copies of each piece of the pattern.

2 **Gather the Tools.** You need the following tools: a straight line ruler with 1/8" interval markings, a seam gauge and a pencil. And, of course, a good pair of craft shears for cutting the paper patterns.

Printing Instructions

*P*lease make sure your printer's scaling is set to "none," "actual size" or "100%". Do NOT check the "scale to fit paper size" option. Once the pattern is printed out, make sure it printed correctly. Check the "1 inch Square" and it should measure 1" x 1". If the square is not the correct size, check the printer settings again.

DIRECTIONS

3 *Add Seam Allowance.* You should have 2 copies of the paper patterns, put one copy aside. Since the pattern does NOT have seam allowance, we need to add seam allowance around the pattern before cutting the fabric.

★ Add seam allowance: 1/4", 3/8" or 1/2" around the paper pattern, to your preference. (refer to the pictures below)

Use the Seam Gauge to draw the seam allowance on the curve area; use the Straight Line Ruler to draw the seam allowance on the straight line. Extend the center markings or other markings to the seam allowance as well.

DIRECTIONS

4 *Cut the pattern.* Cut both patterns out using craft scissors: one with seam allowance and the other without. Now, you should have cutouts of the patterns above.

The pattern with seam allowance is used for cutting the fabric (main and lining).

The pattern without seam allowance is used for cutting the interfacing.

With Seam Allowance

Without Seam Allowance

Understand the Pattern

1 *The Katy - Ava.* I like to name my patterns by using pretty names. "Katy" is the whole set of patterns made with the 3.35" Arch Frame in this book. "Ava" is a subcategory of the "Katy" set, giving each pattern its own name.

2 *3.35" (8.5 cm) Arch Purse Frame.* This means the purse frame size (3.35" or 8.5 cm) and arch shape (Half Round or Oval). Do NOT install the wrong size or shape purse frame to the project.

Understand the Pattern

③ **I_R_V1.** This line consists of three separate parts: "I", "R", and "V1". What do they mean?

I indicates the number of piece(s) required to construct the purse piece (indicated as roman numerals). In this example, you only need to cut out ONE piece as shown.

R means the frame shape. Even though the size says 3.35" Arch, different manufacturers might have the same size in different shapes. In this book, I will use two shapes: Round and Oval. In this example, R means **R**ound shaped, and O means **O**val shaped. Do NOT install the wrong shaped frame onto the purse piece, otherwise you won't get the expected result.

V V1 means "variation 1". I provide more than one variation for most of the patterns in this book. This example shows **V**ariation **1**.

DIRECTIONS

Understand the Pattern

④ Front & Back. This tells you where to connect and construct the purse piece. "Front & Back" means the purse "Front" and/or "Back"; "Side Gusset" means the side of the purse; "Bottom" means the bottom of the purse.

⑤ Seam Allowance. All the patterns provided in this book have NO SEAM ALLOWANCE. Because of this, we will require two sets of the pattern: one without seam allowance (Pattern A) and one with seam allowance drawn in (Pattern B). To make sure you don't mix up the two, circle "_**No Seam Allowance**_" on "_Pattern A_" and "_**Seam Allowance**_" on "_Pattern B_". These patterns will be explained in further detail in the instructions.

⑥ Arrow Markings. The arrow on the pattern indicate direction. If you are using directional fabric, you need to make sure that it's facing the correct direction. Some of the patterns only need one piece of fabric, but with directional fabric, two pieces must be cut and connected to each other.

⑦ Markings. There are markings in all the patterns. You have to transfer them **ALL** to the fabric's seam allowance. These will guide you while sewing two pieces of fabric together. You may use a craft knife or chalk to mark them onto the fabric.

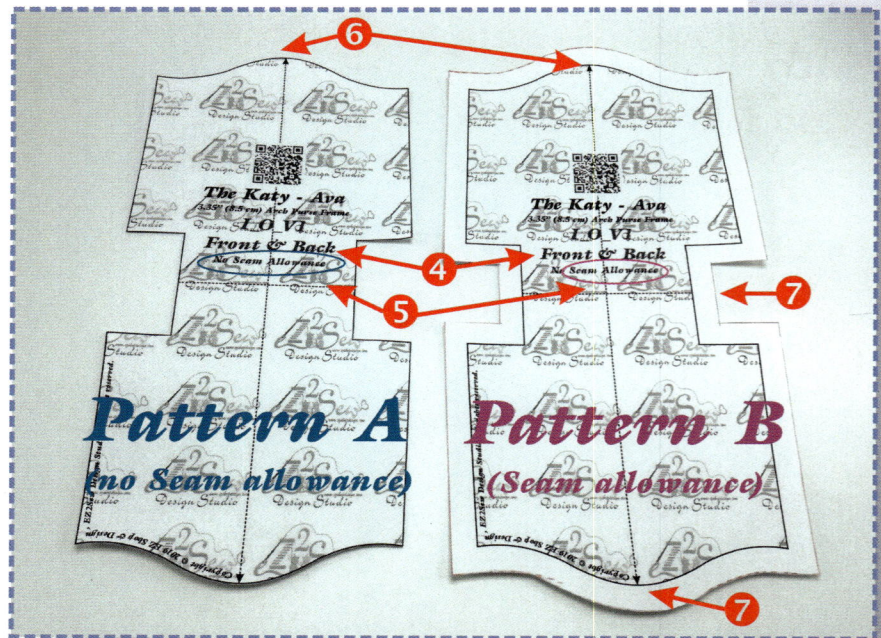

DIRECTIONS

How to Modify the Pattern

*I*f you are (1) using the directional fabric, or (2) would like a taller or wider size or maybe (3) make patchwork, add lace, then you might want to know how to make modifications to the pattern that fit your needs. Here's some basic information on how to do it, however not every pattern provided in this book is modifiable. I will use the "Ava" pattern as an example to explain.

1 *Directional Fabric.* The arrow sign(s) on the pattern indicate the "top" of the purse piece. If the fabric has direction, cutting it regularly will result in one side being upside-down.

To avoid this from happening, we need to fold the original Pattern A (no seam allowance) in half at the center on the horizontal line (Figure 1). Then, trace the new Pattern A onto another sheet of paper, and add the seam allowance around the new Pattern A. This will become your new Pattern B.

The Katy - *Ava*
3.35" (8.5 cm) Arch Purse Frame
I.O.VI
Front & Back
No Seam Allowance

FOLD HERE → ← **FOLD HERE**

Pattern A

*** This is not an actual size pattern, do NOT use this to cut the fabric. ***

Figure 1

Pattern B (new)

Pattern A (new)

← **SEW HERE** →

Figure 2

In using non-directional fabric, only 1 piece of Pattern B is needed, but if you use directional fabric, you need 2 pieces of the new Pattern B and connect both pieces at the bottom to become ONE as shown on the left (Figure 2).

DIRECTIONS

How to Modify the Pattern

2 **Change Size.** Let's say you wanted the final piece 1" taller, wider, or deeper than the original one.

How to add 1" in Height on the pattern

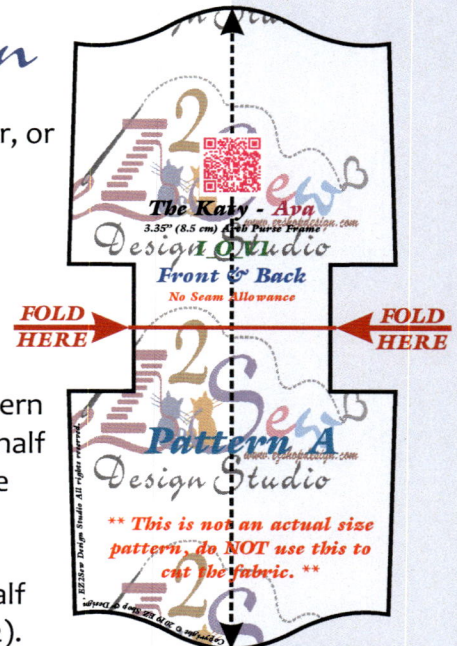

Figure 1

Figure 2

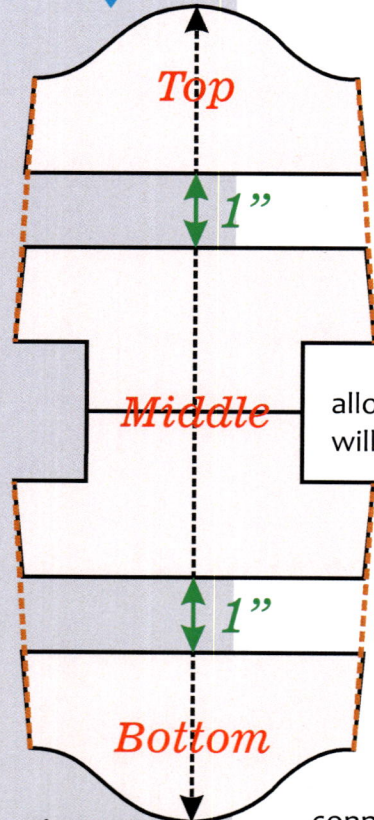

Pattern A
(original, fold in 1/2)

Top

1"

Middle

1"

Bottom

Figure 3

❶ Let's fold the original Pattern A (no seam allowance) in half at the center of the horizontal line (Figure 1).

❷ Then, cut the folded piece in half horizontally as shown (Figure 2). Now, you should have three pieces of the original Pattern A - let's call them "Top, Middle and Bottom".

❸ We need to add 1" between both **Top and Middle** and **Middle and Bottom** (Figure 3).

❹ Trace the new Pattern A to another sheet of paper and add the seam allowance around the new Pattern A. Now, you will have a new Pattern B which has the seam allowance (Figure 4).

❺ Again, if you use non-directional fabric, you need to cut 1 piece of the new Pattern B, but if you use directional fabric, you need to fold the new Pattern B in half (refer to page 36, Figure 2), cut 2 pieces of it and connect both pieces to become ONE piece.

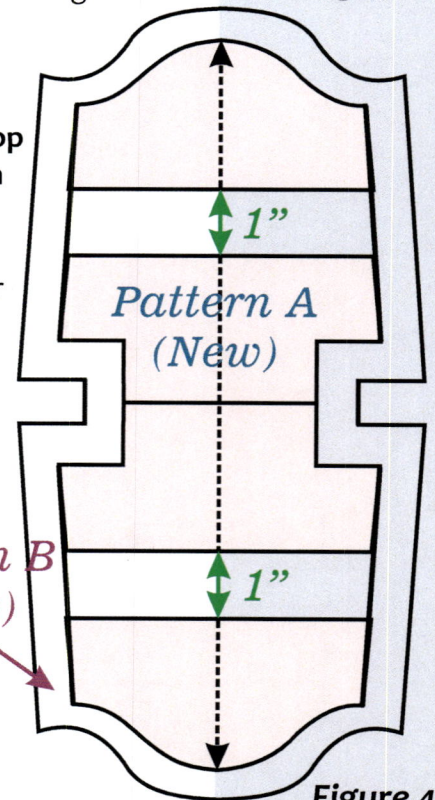

1"

Pattern A
(New)

Pattern B
(New)

1"

Figure 4

DIRECTIONS

How to Modify the Pattern

How to add 1" in Width on the pattern

1 Let's fold the original Pattern A (no seam allowance) in half at the center of the horizontal line (Figure 1).

2 Then, place the folded Pattern A on a blank sheet of paper and add 0.5" on each side of the folded Pattern A at labels ① and ② (Figure 2).

3 Connect the extension to the top two corners of the pattern and trace the rest. We currently have half of the new Pattern A (with 1" additional width). Do the same with the other half to make the new Pattern A.

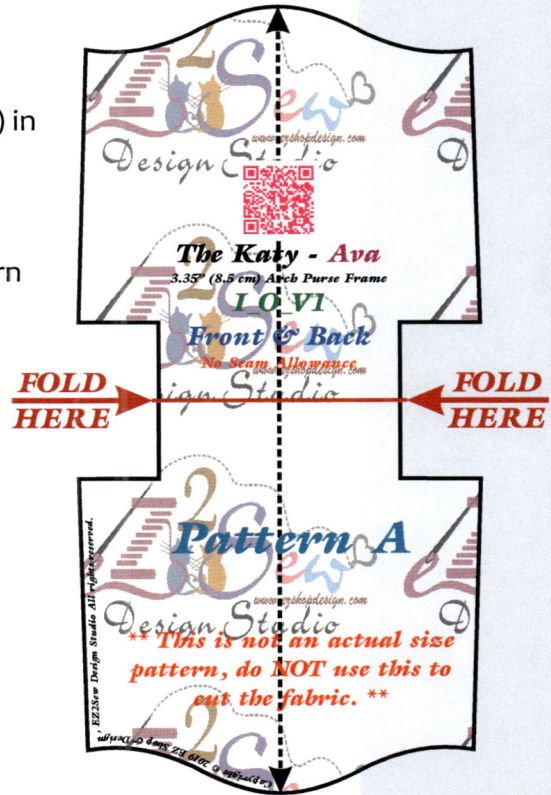

Figure 1

4 Add seam allowance around the new Pattern A. This will be your new Pattern B.

5 Again, if you use non-directional fabric, you need to cut 1 piece of the new Pattern B, but if you use directional fabric, you need to fold the new Pattern B in half (refer to page 36, Figure 2), cut 2 pieces of it and connect both pieces to become ONE piece.

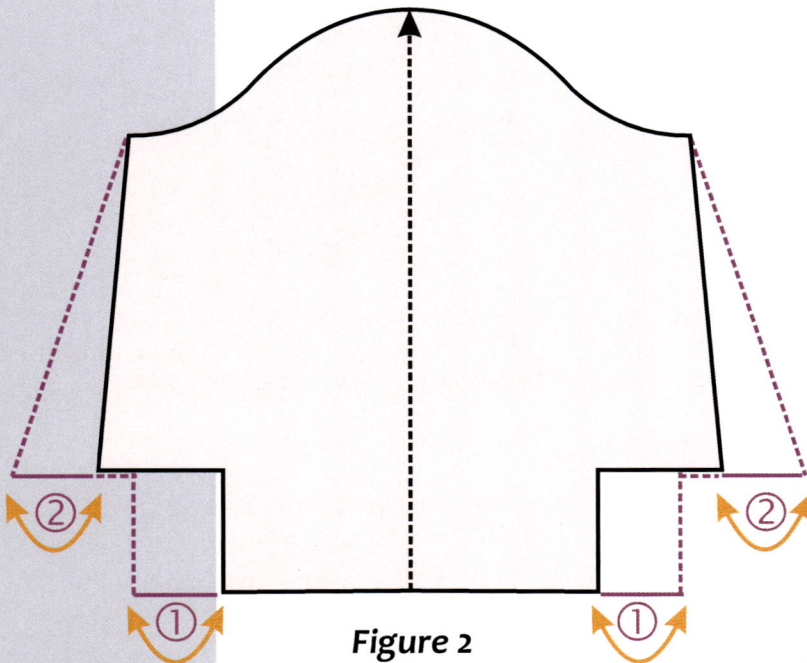

Figure 2

DIRECTIONS

How to Modify the Pattern

How to add 1" in Depth on the pattern

1 Let's fold the original Pattern A (no seam allowance) in half at the center of the horizontal line (Figure 1).

2 Then, place the folded Pattern A on a blank sheet of paper and add 0.5" on each side at labels ③ and ④ (Figure 2).

3 Using a ruler, connect the extensions and trace the rest of the pattern. Now we should have half of the new Pattern A with the additional 1" in depth. Do the same with the other half to complete the new Pattern A.

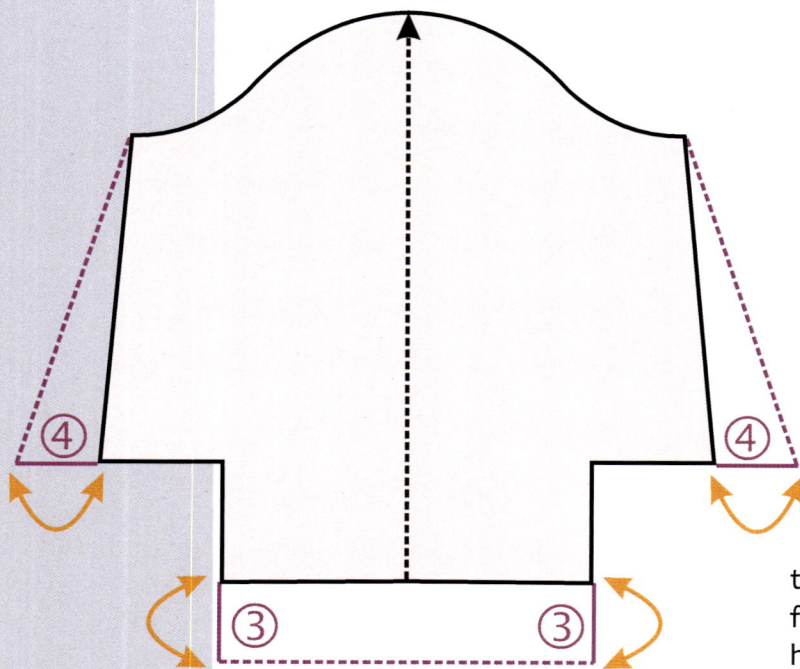

The Katy - Ava
3,35" (8.5 cm) Arch Purse Frame
L_R_V1
Front & Back
No Seam Allowance
FOLD HERE → ← FOLD HERE
Pattern A
This is not an actual size pattern, do NOT use this to cut the fabric.

Figure 1

Figure 2

4 Add seam allowance around the new Pattern A. This will be your new Pattern B.

5 Again, if you use non-directional fabric, you need to cut 1 piece of the new Pattern B, but if you use directional fabric, you need to fold the new Pattern B in half (refer to page 36, Figure 2), cut 2 pieces of it and connect both pieces to become ONE piece.

DIRECTIONS

How to Modify the Pattern

3 **Patchwork.** Some of the patterns require more than one piece to construct the purse, so adding contrasting fabric to the finished project is possible. How about the ONE piece patterns, like the "Ava"?

If you prefer the simple approach, you can still use a single piece of fabric to construct the project. But if you want to add patchwork, add contrasting pieces at the bottom, or add lace, it's easy. Just follow the steps below. For the bottom, I have included the "Bottom" for the ONE piece patterns if you don't want to create your own (Figure 2).

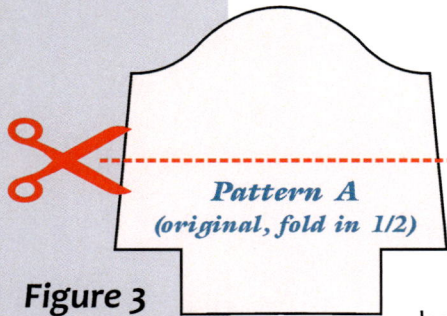

Figure 1

The Katy - *Ava*
3.35" (8.5 cm) Arch Purse Frame
I R V I
Front & Back
No Seam Allowance

FOLD HERE → ← FOLD HERE

Pattern A

** *This is not an actual size pattern, do NOT use this to cut the fabric*

❶ Fold the original Pattern A (Front & Back, no seam allowance) in half at the center of the horizontal line (Figure 1).

Pattern A
(original, fold in 1/2)

Figure 3

❷ Then, cut anywhere you would like to divide, for instance, 2" from the top or 1.5" from the bottom, horizontally as shown (Figure 3). Now, you should have three pieces of the original Pattern A, 2 "Top"s and 1 "Bottom". These three pieces will become your new Pattern A.

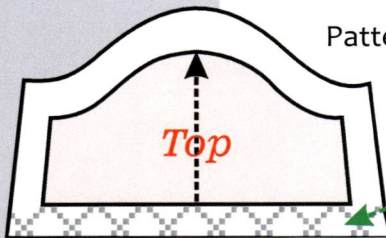

Figure 2

The Katy - *Ava*
3.35" (8.5 cm) Arch Purse Frame
I o v e
Bottom
No Seam Allowance

Top

Figure 4

doL

Bottom

❸ Add seam allowance all the way around to the new Pattern A-Top and A-Bottom. Then you will have the new Pattern B-Top and B-Bottom (Figure 4).

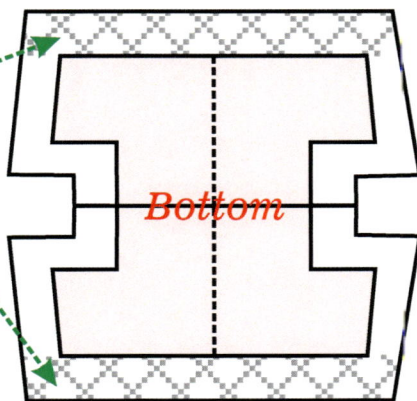

❹ Use the new Pattern B to cut the fabric. Place the Top and Bottom pieces Right side facing each other (add lace in between if you like), and sew the Top and Bottom together with the seam allowance of your choice. These three pieces will become ONE piece after being sewn together.

The Katy
One piece, Oval shape frame

Brooklyn

Ava

Ava

The Katy - *Ava (I_O_V1)*

- **ONE-piece**
- **Oval Shape Frame**
- **Variation 1**

Finished Size: (approximate measurements)

4" (Top W) x 3" (Bottom W)
4" (H) x 2" (D)

* Top W: the widest part; H: not including the frame;

NOTE:

The attached pattern has __NO__ seam allowances included. Refer to the Chapter "How to Use The Pattern" completely before cutting or sewing! ☺

Fabric Cuts:

If you are using directional fabric, please make sure they are facing in the right direction.

Tips: *(1) Print 2 copies of the pattern or trace the pattern onto blank paper, (2) add seam allowances to your preference (1/4", 3/8" or 1/2") around one of the patterns, (3) transfer all the markings, (4) cut out the pattern without (Pattern A) and with (Pattern B) seam allowances.*

SEWING SKILL

★ *Beginner* ★☆☆☆☆

DIFFICULT LEVEL

★ *Very Easy* ●○○○○

Lining

Main

PREPARING ALL THE MATERIALS

✂ For NON-Directional Fabrics

Exterior/Interfacing:

- **Main** fabric - "Front & Back" (Pattern B) x 1;

- **Interfacing** - "Front & Back" (Pattern A) x 1; (no seam allowance needed)

Interior/Interfacing:

- **Lining** fabric - "Front & Back" (Pattern B) x 1;

- **Interfacing** - "Front & Back" (Pattern A) x 1; (no seam allowance needed)

✂ For Directional Fabrics

Exterior/Interfacing:

- **Main** fabric - "Front & Back" (Pattern B) x 2;

- ✂ **Patchwork:** "Top" (Pattern B) x 2; "Bottom" (Pattern B) x 1; Optional: Lace x 2;

- **Interfacing** - "Front & Back" (Pattern A) x 1; (no seam allowance needed)

*Tip: Do **NOT** apply the interfacing until all the Main pieces are connected together and become ONE piece.*

Interior/Interfacing:

- **Lining** fabric - "Front & Back" (Pattern B) x 2;

- **Interfacing** - "Front & Back" (Pattern A) x 1; (no seam allowance needed)

Reference

- ★ *For cutting the* **Directional fabrics** - *please refer to the Chapter* ˮ**How to Use The Pattern**ˮ
- ★ **Pattern A** - *the original pattern which has* **ˮNO Seam Allowanceˮ**
- ★ **Pattern B** - *the pattern which has the* **ˮSeam Allowanceˮ** *of your choice (1/4ˮ, 3/8ˮ or 1/2ˮ)*

DIRECTIONS

For Directional Fabrics

The following steps are for those who will be using directional fabrics and/or making patchwork. If you are using non-directonal fabrics and don't want to make patchwork, you may skip these steps.

Construct the Exterior

1 **Cut the fabrics.** Please refer to the Chapter "How to Use The Pattern", under the Section "How to Modify the Pattern" - "1. Directional Fabric" and "3. Patchwork".

2 **Connect the fabrics together.**

☞ If you cut the fabric in 2 pieces - 2 x "Front & Back": Connect both pieces at the bottom, Right side facing together. Sew by using the seam allowance of your choice.

☞ If you cut the fabric in 3 pieces - 2 x "Top" and 1 x "Bottom": Place the bottom of the "Top" and one of the flat edges of the "Bottom", right side facing each other. If you want to add lace, put it in between the two pieces and sew by using the seam allowance of your choice.

3 **Press seam allowances open.** Press seam allowances open flat at the Wrong side. The lace can be placed upward or downward, depending on the lace you use and if the lace has direction. Now the Exterior is ONE piece.

① "Bottom" / Lining / "Top"

② "Top" / "Bottom"

③ *Press seam allowances open*

DIRECTIONS

Construct the Exterior

4 **Get the fabrics ready.** You should have one piece of Main/Exterior, one piece of Lining/Interior and both interfacings ready.

5 **Fusing the fabrics.** Apply interfacing to the Wrong side of the main and lining fabrics, following the manufacturer's instructions. Please refer to the Section "Apply Interfacing" for more details.

*For those who use directional fabric and/or make patchwork, you may top stitch 1/8" or 1/16" away from the connecting edge **AFTER** applying the interfacing to the fabric.*

Construct the Exterior

6 **Fold the Main fabric in half.** Fold the Main fabric in half, Right side facing together; Align all the markings, top-centers and bottom-centers.

Use pins or clips to hold them in place. Make sure all the markings are aligned.

7 **Sew both sides.** Sew both sides by using the seam allowance of your choice. Press open the side seam allowances.

8 **Sew box corners.** Fold the box corner, align the center of the side seam and the center marking of the bottom; sew both box corners by using the seam allowance of your choice.

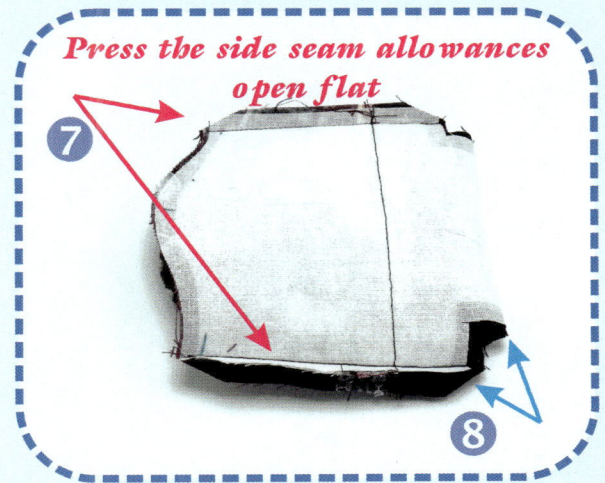

Fold Here

Press the side seam allowances open flat

DIRECTIONS

Construct the Exterior

9 **Turn the Main piece.** We just completed constructing the Main piece. Turn it Right side out and put it aside.

Construct the Interior

1 **Fold the Lining fabric in half.** Fold the Lining fabric in half, Right side facing together; Align all the markings, top-centers and bottom-centers.

2 **Sew both sides.** Sew both sides by using the seam allowance of your choice. Press open the side seam allowances.

LEAVE AN OPENING on either side along the **straight** seam for turning the whole piece Right side out later.

3 **Sew box corners.** Fold the box corner, align the center of the side seam and the center marking of the bottom; sew both box corners by using the seam allowance of your choice.

Fold Here

DIRECTIONS

Complete the Purse piece

1 **Get Main and Lining pieces. Connect both pieces.** You should have both Main and Lining pieces ready to complete the purse piece. Place the Main piece (Right side out) into the Lining piece (Wrong side out), with the Right sides of both pieces facing each other. Align all 4 center markings.

Use chalk or erasable pen to draw the seam line on the Wrong side of the Lining before sewing.

2 **Sew all the way around.** Sew all the way around the top to connect both pieces with the seam allowance of your choice. Use Pinking Shears to trim the excess or cut notches on the curved seam. Clip the tops of both side seams.

3 **Turn Right side out.** Turn the whole purse piece Right side out through the opening. Use your finger tip or something pointy (but not sharp) to round out the top curved seam.

4 **Press well.** Use an iron to press the purse piece with a bit of steam to remove wrinkles if necessary.

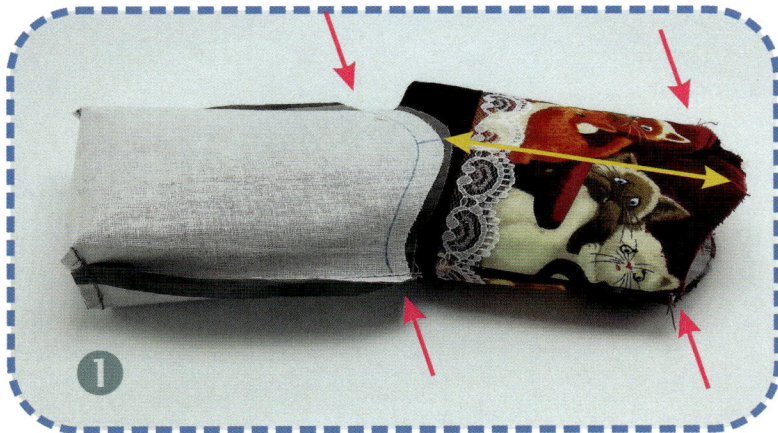

DIRECTIONS

Complete the Purse piece

5 **Close the opening.** Use Ladder/Blind stitches to close the opening.

6 **Top stitch.** Top stitch all the way around the top edge by using 1/16" seam allowance.

Do NOT use a seam allowance larger than 1/8", even though the top edge will be under the frame; using a seam allowance smaller than 1/8" will work well.

7 **Mark all 4 centers.** Press well if needed. Use chalk or erasable pen to mark all 4 centers.

Install the purse frame

1 **Install the purse frame.** Get the correct size and shape purse frame ready to install to the completed purse piece.

Please refer to the Chapter "Install Sew-In Purse Frame".

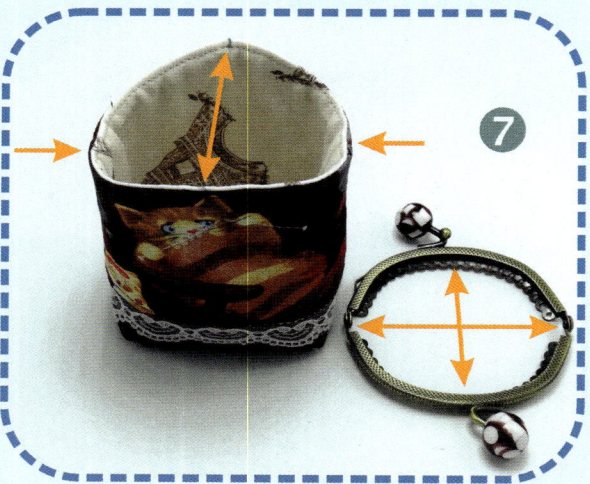

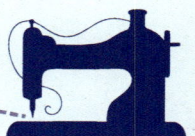

3.35" Oval

The Katy - *Ava*

3.35" (8.5 cm) Arch Purse Frame

LO_V1

Front & Back

No Seam Allowance

1"

The Katy - *Ava*

3.35" (8.5 cm) Arch Purse Frame

I O V1

Bottom

No Seam Allowance

1"

The Katy - *Brooklyn*

3.35" (8.5 cm) Arch Purse Frame

I O V2

Bottom

No Seam Allowance

The Katy - Brooklyn

3.35" (8.5 cm) Arch Purse Frame

L_0_V2

Front & Back

No Seam Allowance

1"

yn oval

(1_O_V2)

#of Pieces

- **ONE-piece**
- **Oval Shape Frame**
- **Variation 2**

Finished Size: (approximate measurements)

4" (Top W) x 3" (Bottom W)
3.25" (H) x 2" (D)

* Top W: the widest part; H: not including the frame;

NOTE:

The attached pattern has __NO__ seam allowances included. Refer to the Chapter "How to Use The Pattern" completely before cutting or sewing! ☺

Fabric Cuts:

If you are using directional fabric, please make sure they are facing in the right direction.

Tips: *(1) Print 2 copies of the pattern or trace the pattern onto blank paper, (2) add seam allowances to your preference (1/4", 3/8" or 1/2") around one of the patterns, (3) transfer all the markings, (4) cut out the pattern without (Pattern A) and with (Pattern B) seam allowances.*

SEWING SKILL

★ *Beginner* ★☆☆☆☆

DIFFICULT LEVEL

★ *Very Easy* ●○○○○

The Katy

One piece, Round shape frame

Daisy

Evelyn

Charlotte

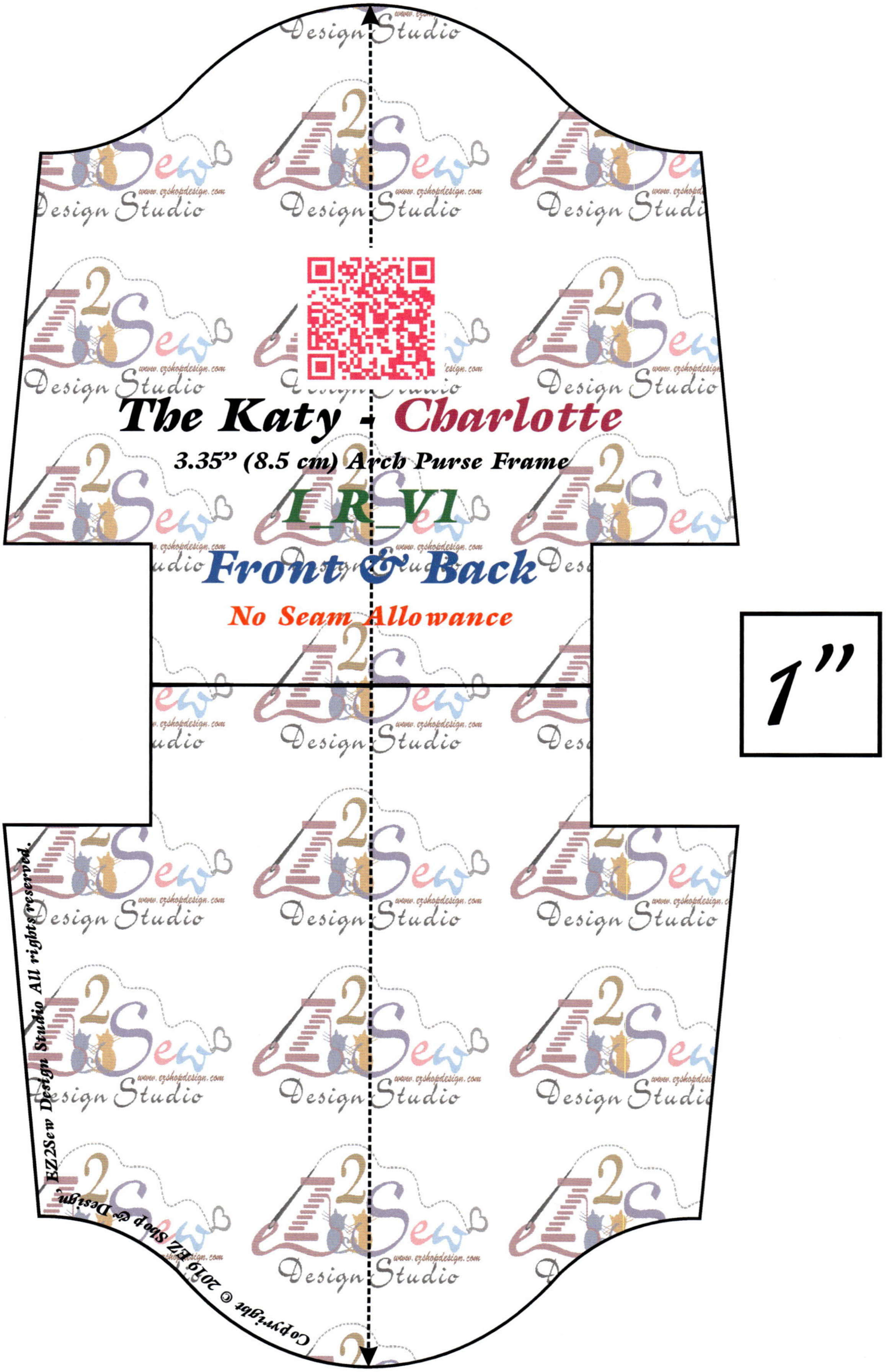

The Katy - Charlotte
3.35” (8.5 cm) Arch Purse Frame
I_R_V1
Front & Back
No Seam Allowance
1”
Copyright © 2019 EZ Shop & Design, EZ2Sew Design Studio All rights reserved.

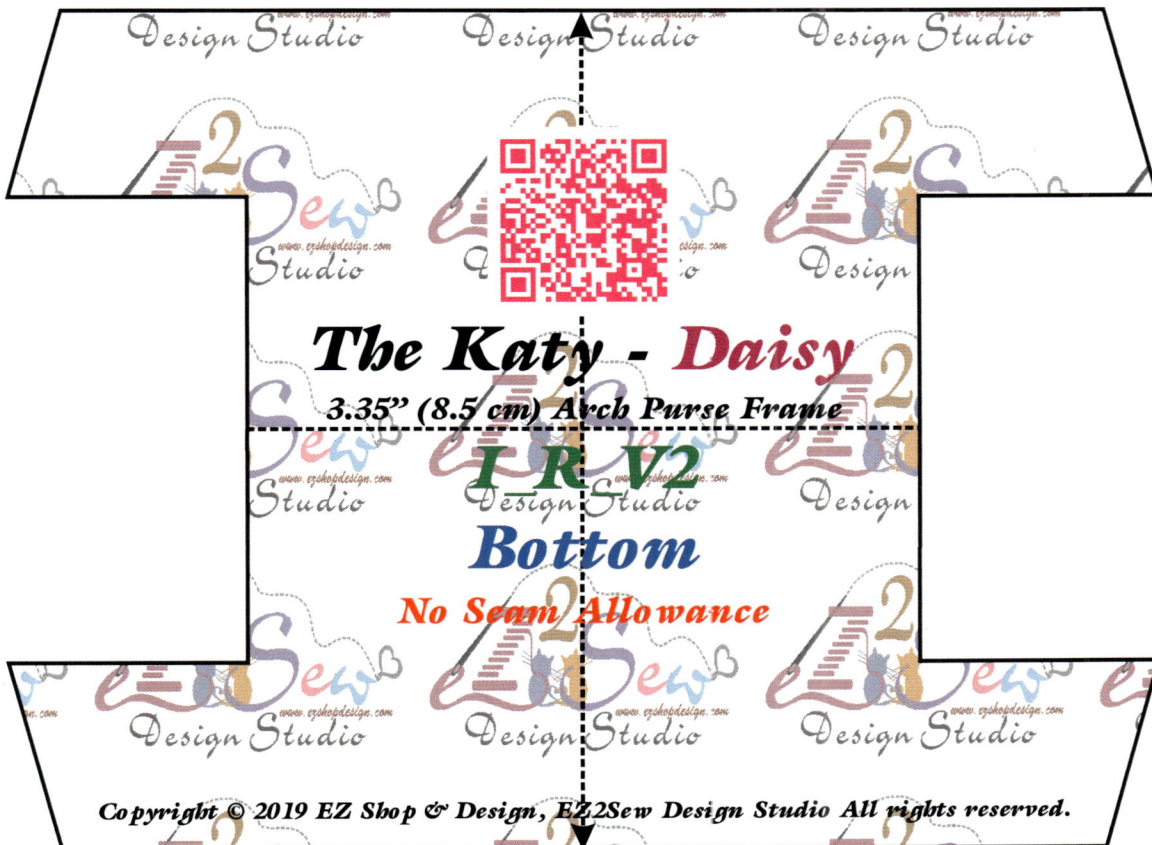

The Katy - Charlotte
3.35" (8.5 cm) Arch Purse Frame
I_R_V1
Bottom
No Seam Allowance

1"

The Katy - Daisy
3.35" (8.5 cm) Arch Purse Frame
I_R_V2
Bottom
No Seam Allowance

The Katy-*Daisy*

3.35" (8.5 cm) Arch Purse Frame

I_R_V2

Front & Back

No Seam Allowance

1"

Charlotte

The Katy - Charlotte (I_R_V1)

- **ONE-piece**
- **Round Shape Frame**
- **Variation 1**

Finished Size: (approximate measurements)

3.5" (Top W) x 3" (Bottom W)
3.75" (H) x 2" (D)

* Top W: the widest part; H: not including the frame;

NOTE:

*The attached pattern has **NO** seam allowances included. Refer to the Chapter "How to Use The Pattern" completely before cutting or sewing!* ☺

Fabric Cuts:

If you are using directional fabric, please make sure they are facing in the right direction.

Tips: *(1) Print 2 copies of the pattern or trace the pattern onto blank paper, (2) add seam allowances to your preference (1/4", 3/8" or 1/2") around one of the patterns, (3) transfer all the markings, (4) cut out the pattern without (Pattern A) and with (Pattern B) seam allowances.*

SEWING SKILL

★ *Beginner* ★☆☆☆☆

DIFFICULT LEVEL

★ *Very Easy* ●○○○○

PREPARING ALL THE MATERIALS

✂ For NON-Directional Fabrics

Exterior/Interfacing:

- **Main** fabric - "Front & Back" (Pattern B) x 1;

- **Interfacing** - "Front & Back" (Pattern A) x 1; (no seam allowance needed)

Interior/Interfacing:

- **Lining** fabric - "Front & Back" (Pattern B) x 1;

- **Interfacing** - "Front & Back" (Pattern A) x 1; (no seam allowance needed)

✂ For Directional Fabrics

Exterior/Interfacing:

- **Main** fabric - "Front & Back" (Pattern B) x 2;

- ✂ **Patchwork:** "Top" (Pattern B) x 2; "Bottom" (Pattern B) x 1; Optional: Lace x 2;

- **Interfacing** - "Front & Back" (Pattern A) x 1; (no seam allowance needed)

*Tip: Do **NOT** apply the interfacing until all the Main pieces are connected together and become ONE piece.*

Interior/Interfacing:

- **Lining** fabric - "Front & Back" (Pattern B) x 2;

- **Interfacing** - "Front & Back" (Pattern A) x 1; (no seam allowance needed)

Lining

Main

Reference

★ *For cutting the **Directional fabrics** - please refer to the Chapter "**How to Use The Pattern**"*

★ **_Pattern A_** *- the original pattern which has "**NO Seam Allowance**"*

★ **_Pattern B_** *- the pattern which has the "**Seam Allowance**" of your choice (1/4", 3/8" or 1/2")*

DIRECTIONS

For Directional Fabrics

The following steps are for those who will be using directional fabrics and/or making patchwork. If you are using non-directonal fabrics and don't want to make patchwork, you may skip these steps.

Construct the Exterior

1 **Cut the fabrics.** Please refer to the Chapter "How to Use The Pattern", under the Section "How to Modify the Pattern" - "1. Directional Fabric" and "3. Patchwork".

2 **Connect the fabrics together.**

☞ If you cut the fabric in 2 pieces - 2 x "Front & Back": Connect both pieces at the bottom, Right side facing together. Sew by using the seam allowance of your choice.

☞ If you cut the fabric in 3 pieces - 2 x "Top" and 1 x "Bottom": Place the bottom of the "Top" and one of the flat edges of the "Bottom", right side facing each other. If you want to add lace, put it in between the two pieces and sew by using the seam allowance of your choice.

3 **Press the seam allowances open.** Press seam allowances open flat at the Wrong side. The lace can be placed upward or downward, depending on the lace you use and if the lace has direction. Now the Exterior is ONE piece.

"Top"

"Bottom"

Press seam allowances open

DIRECTIONS

Construct the Exterior

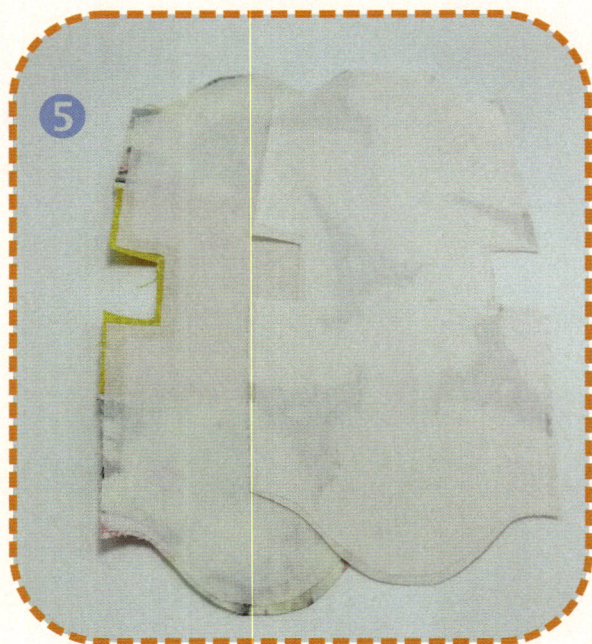

4 Get the fabrics ready. You should have one piece of Main/Exterior, one piece of Lining/Interior and both interfacings ready.

5 Fusing the fabrics. Apply interfacing to the Wrong side of the main and lining fabrics, following the manufacturer's instructions. Please refer to the Section "Apply Interfacing" for more details.

*For those who use directional fabric and/or make patchwork, you may top stitch 1/8" or 1/16" away from the connecting edge **AFTER** applying the interfacing to the fabric.*

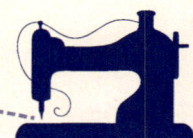

DIRECTIONS

Construct the Exterior

6 **Fold the Main fabric in half.** Fold the Main fabric in half, Right side facing together; Align all the markings, top-centers and bottom-centers.

Use pins or clips to hold them in place. Make sure all the markings are aligned.

7 **Sew both sides.** Sew both sides by using the seam allowance of your choice. Press open the side seam allowances.

8 **Sew box corners.** Fold the box corner, align the center of the side seam and the center marking of the bottom; sew both box corners by using the seam allowance of your choice.

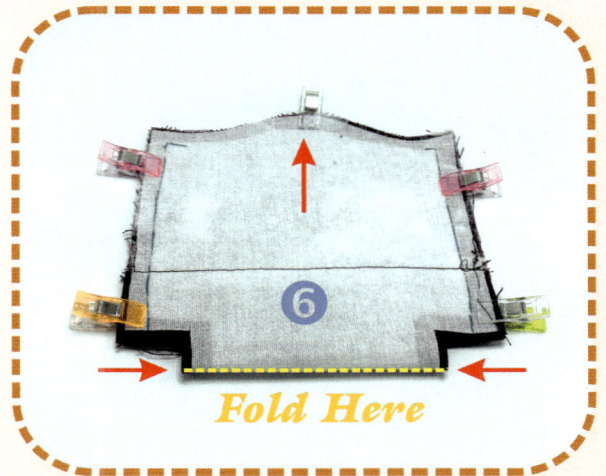

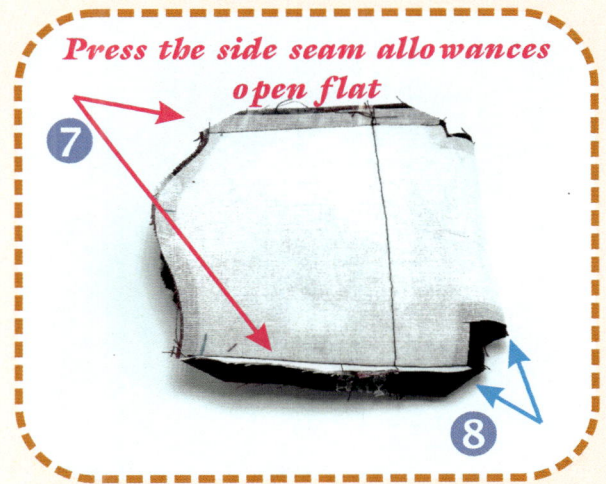

6

Fold Here

7

7

Press the side seam allowances open flat

8

8

DIRECTIONS

Fold Here

Construct the Exterior

9 **Turn the Main piece.** We just completed constructing the Main piece. Turn it Right side out and put it aside.

Construct the Interior

1 **Fold the Lining fabric in half.** Fold the Lining fabric in half, Right side facing together; Align all the markings, top-centers and bottom-centers.

2 **Sew both sides.** Sew both sides by using the seam allowance of your choice. Press open the side seam allowances.

LEAVE AN OPENING on either side along the **straight** *seam for turning the whole piece Right side out later.*

3 **Sew box corners.** Fold the box corner, align the center of the side seam and the center marking of the bottom; sew both box corners by using the seam allowance of your choice.

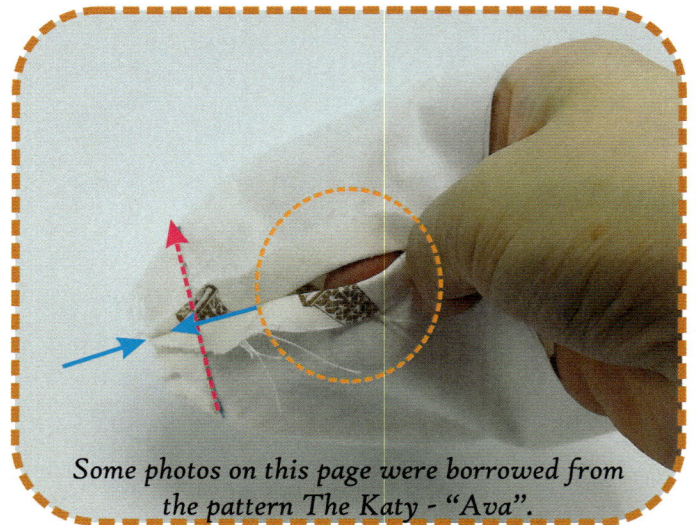

Some photos on this page were borrowed from the pattern The Katy - "Ava".

DIRECTIONS

Complete the Purse piece

1 **Get Main and Lining pieces. Connect both pieces.** You should have both Main and Lining pieces ready to complete the purse piece. Place the Main piece (Right side out) into the Lining piece (Wrong side out), with the Right sides of both pieces facing each other. Align all 4 center markings.

Use chalk or erasable pen to draw the seam line on the Wrong side of the Lining before sewing.

2 **Sew all the way around.** Sew all the way around the top to connect both pieces with the seam allowance of your choice. Use Pinking Shears to trim the excess or cut notches on the curved seam. Clip the tops of both side seams.

3 **Turn Right side out.** Turn the whole purse piece Right side out through the opening. Use your finger tip or something pointy (but not sharp) to round out the top curved seam.

4 **Press well.** Use an iron to press the purse piece with a bit of steam to remove wrinkles if necessary.

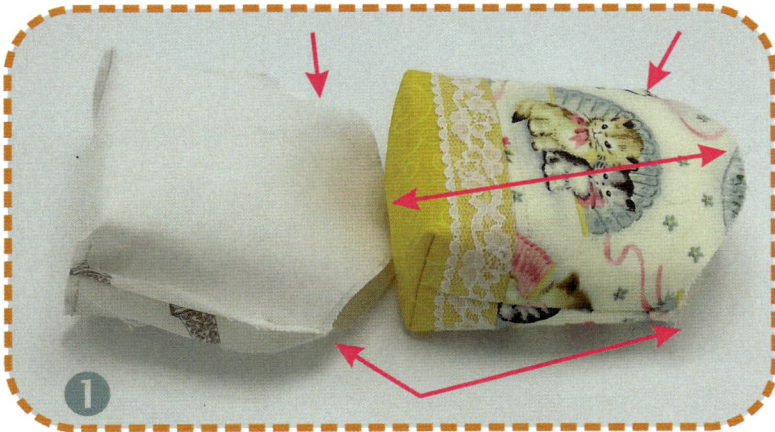

DIRECTIONS

Complete the Purse piece

5 Close the opening. Use Ladder/Blind stitches to close the opening.

6 Top Stitch. Top Stitch all the way around the top edge by using 1/16" seam allowance.

Do NOT use a seam allowance larger than 1/8", even though the top edge will be under the frame; using a seam allowance smaller than 1/8" will work well.

7 Mark all 4 centers. Press well if needed. Use chalk or erasable pen to mark all 4 centers.

Install the purse frame

1 Install the purse frame. Get the correct size and shape purse frame ready to install to the completed purse piece.

Please refer to the Chapter "Install Sew-In Purse Frame".

3.35" Round

Some photos on this page were borrowed from the pattern The Katy - "Ava".

Daisy

The Katy - Daisy (I_R_V2)

- **ONE-piece**
- **Round Shape Frame**
- **Variation 2**

Finished Size: (approximate measurements)

4.25" (Top W) x 3.5" (Bottom W)
3.75" (H) x 2.5" (D)

* Top W: the widest part; H: not including the frame;

NOTE:

*The attached pattern has **NO** seam allowances included. Refer to the Chapter "How to Use The Pattern" completely before cutting or sewing!* ☺

Fabric Cuts:

If you are using directional fabric, please make sure they are facing in the right direction.

Tips: *(1) Print 2 copies of the pattern or trace the pattern onto blank paper, (2) add seam allowances to your preference (1/4", 3/8" or 1/2") around one of the patterns, (3) transfer all the markings, (4) cut out the pattern without (Pattern A) and with (Pattern B) seam allowances.*

SEWING SKILL

★ *Beginner* ★☆☆☆☆

DIFFICULT LEVEL

★ *Very Easy* ●○○○○

** *Please refer to the pattern, "Charlotte", for instructions on how to construct this pattern.* **

Evelyn

The Katy - Evelyn (I_R_V3)

- **ONE-piece**
- **Round Shape Frame**
- **Variation 3**

Finished Size: (approximate measurements)

4" (Top W) x 3" (Bottom W)
3.75" (H) x 2.5" (D)

* Top W: the widest part; H: not including the frame;

NOTE:

*The attached pattern has **NO** seam allowances included. Refer to the Chapter "How to Use The Pattern" completely before cutting or sewing!* ☺

Fabric Cuts:

If you are using directional fabric, please make sure they are facing in the right direction.

Tips: *(1) Print 2 copies of the pattern or trace the pattern onto blank paper, (2) add seam allowances to your preference (1/4", 3/8" or 1/2") around one of the patterns, (3) transfer all the markings, (4) cut out the pattern without (Pattern A) and with (Pattern B) seam allowances.*

SEWING SKILL

★ Beginner ★☆☆☆☆

DIFFICULT LEVEL

★ Very Easy ●○○○○

The Katy - *Evelyn*

3.35" (8.5 cm) Arch Purse Frame

I_R_V3

Front & Back

No Seam Allowance

1"

The Katy - Evelyn

3.35" (8.5 cm) Arch Purse Frame

I_R V3

Bottom

No Seam Allowance

$1''$

Printing Instructions

Please make sure your printer's scaling is set to "none," "actual size" or "100%". Do NOT check the "scale to fit paper size" option. Once the pattern is printed out, make sure it printed correctly. Check the "1 inch Square" and it should measure 1" x 1". If the square is not the correct size, check the printer settings again.

The Katy

Two pieces, *Round* shape frame

Faith

Faith

The Katy - Faith (II_R_V1)

- **TWO-piece**
- **Round Shape Frame**
- **Variation 1**

Finished Size: (approximate measurements)

4" (Top W) x 2" (Bottom W)
3" (H) x 2.25" (D)

* Top W: the widest part; H: not including the frame;

NOTE:

*The attached pattern has **NO** seam allowances included. Refer to the Chapter "How to Use The Pattern" completely before cutting or sewing!* ☺

Fabric Cuts:

If you are using directional fabric, please make sure they are facing in the right direction.

Tips: *(1) Print 2 copies of the pattern or trace the pattern onto blank paper, (2) add seam allowances to your preference (1/4", 3/8" or 1/2") around one of the patterns, (3) transfer all the markings, (4) cut out the pattern without (Pattern A) and with (Pattern B) seam allowances.*

SEWING SKILL

★ *Beginner/Intermediate*

★★☆☆☆

DIFFICULT LEVEL

★ *Intermediate* ●●●○○

PREPARING ALL THE MATERIALS

✂ For NON-Directional Fabrics

Exterior/Interfacing:

- **Main** fabric - "Front & Back" (Pattern B) x 2;

- **Interfacing** - "Front & Back" (Pattern A) x 2; (no seam allowance needed)

Interior/Interfacing:

- **Lining** fabric - "Front & Back" (Pattern B) x 2;

- **Interfacing** - "Front & Back" (Pattern A) x 2; (no seam allowance needed)

✂ For Directional Fabrics

Exterior/Interfacing:

- Main fabric - the same as non-directional fabrics;

- **Interfacing** - the same as above;

✂ Interior/Interfacing:

- **Main** fabric - the same as non-directional fabrics;

- **Interfacing** - the same as above;

Reference

★ For cutting the **Directional fabrics** - please refer to the Chapter "**How to Use The Pattern**"

★ **Pattern A** - the original pattern which has "**NO Seam Allowance**"

★ **Pattern B** - the pattern which has the "**Seam Allowance**" of your choice (1/4", 3/8" or 1/2")

*P*lease refer to the Section "Apply Interfacing" for more details on how to "Apply Single or Double Layer" interfacing.

DIRECTIONS

For Directional Fabrics

There is no difference between cutting directional and non-directional fabrics for this 2-piece pattern. If you are using directional fabrics, make sure they are in the correct direction.

Prepare the Materials

1 **Cut the fabrics and interfacing.** You should have 2 pieces of Main/Exterior (2 x "Front & Back"), 2 pieces of Lining/Interior (2 x "Front & Back") and all the interfacings ready.

2 **Fusing the fabrics.** Apply interfacing to the Wrong side of the main and lining fabrics, following the manufacturer's instructions. Please refer to the Section "Apply Interfacing" for more details.

Main
Interfacing
Lining

❶

Lining
Main

Single Layer Interfacing

Double Layer Interfacing

❷

Note

*I*f you would like a more structured look, you might want to apply two layers of interfacing. If you would like a softer feel, then a single layer of fleece will work.

DIRECTIONS

Construct the Interior

1 **Trace Pattern A on the Wrong side of the fabrics.** Trace Pattern A (with NO seam allowance) to all the pieces on the Wrong side of the fabrics and transfer all the markings as well.

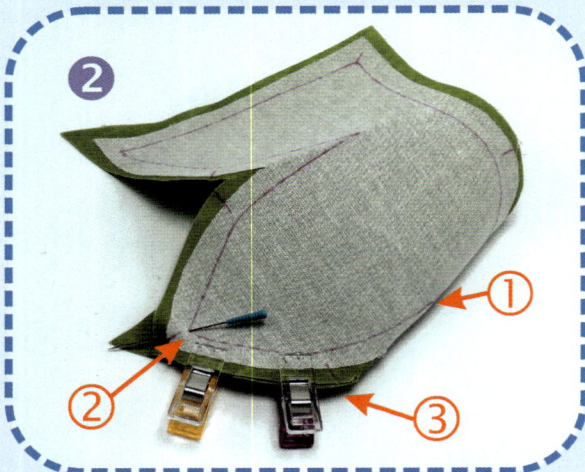

2 **Fold the Curved Dart, Align Markings.** Take one of the "Front & Back" pieces, fold one of the curved darts and line up all the markings, ①, ② and ③.

✏️ *Use pins or clips to hold them in place. Make sure all the markings are aligned.*

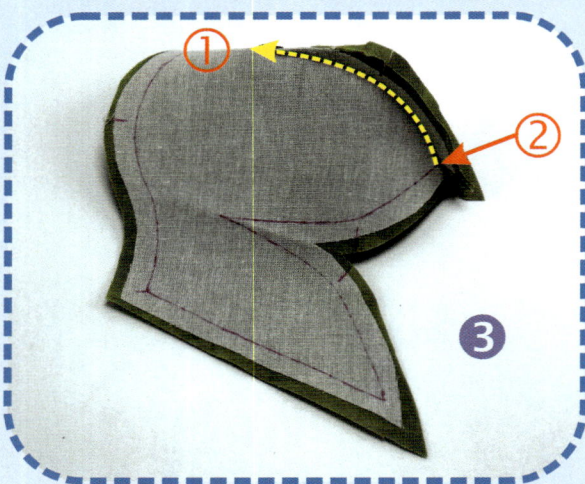

3 **Slowly sew along the marked line.** Sew from ② and stop at ① by using the seam allowance of your choice, do not backstitch after sewing off the fabric, leave a long thread tail. Knot the tail close to the edge. This keeps the thread from coming undone, like backstitching, but do not pull the knot too tight, otherwise it will cause puckering.

✏️ *You may need to sew a little bit slower while sewing the curved dart.*

4 **Repeat Steps 2 and 3.** Repeat steps 2 and 3 on the other curved dart. Join both sides at ②.

DIRECTIONS

Construct the Interior

5 **Repeat Steps 2 to 4.** Repeat steps 2 to 4 on the other "Front & Back" piece.

6 **Join both "Front & Back" pieces.** After step 5, you should have two of the same "Front & Back" pieces. Place both pieces Right side facing each other, matching all the markings, especially the bottom one.

Make sure all the markings are aligned well, if not, the bottom will look crooked. Pin or clip to hold them in place.

7 **Sew all the way around.** Sew all the way around with the seam allowance of your choice. Start from the marking ①, leave an opening, and end at marking ③.

SLOW DOWN while sewing on the curved seam, especially when crossing marking ②.

*LEAVE AN OPENING at the **straight** seam for turning the whole piece Right side out later.*

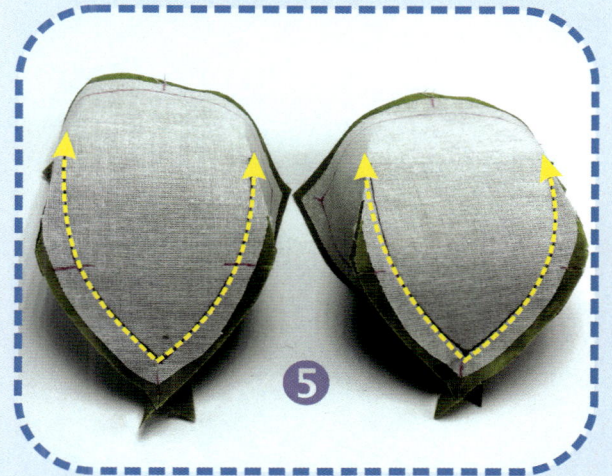

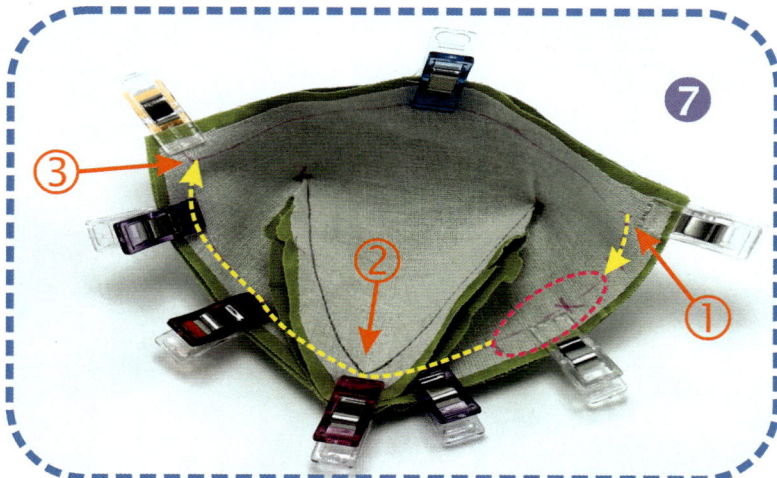

DIRECTIONS

Construct the Interior

8 Make notches and Press well. Cut notches at all the curved seams. Press all the seam allowances open. Trim the excess if necessary. Put aside the completed Lining piece.

Construct the Exterior

1 Construct the exterior using the same process as you did with the lining, except you do NOT need to leave an opening. Sew the exterior by using the seam allowance of your choice.

*NO need to leave an opening. **SEW SLOWLY** on all the curved seams.*

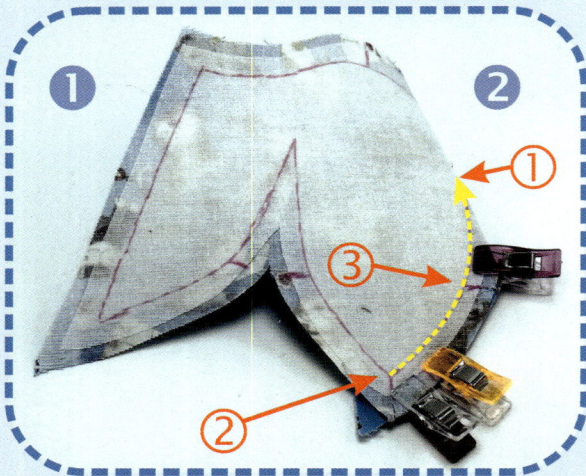

Complete the Purse piece

1 Get both Main and Lining pieces ready to connect. You should have both Main and Lining pieces ready to complete the purse piece. Place the Main piece (Right side out) into the Lining piece (Wrong side out), with the Right sides of both pieces facing each other. Align all 4 center markings.

Use chalk or erasable pen to draw the seam line on the Wrong side of the Lining before sewing.

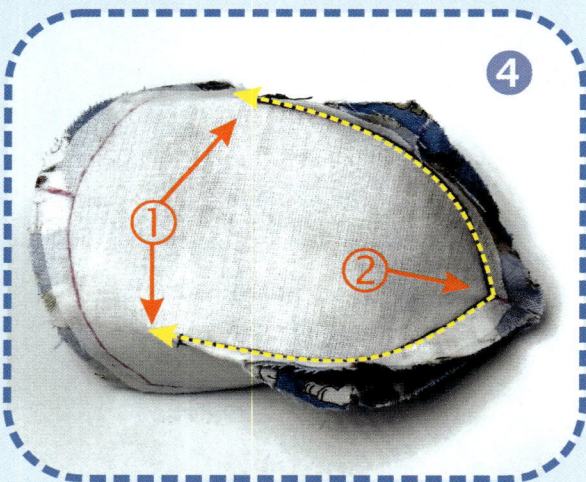

DIRECTIONS

Complete the Purse piece

2 **Sew all the way around.** Sew all the way around the top edge to connect both pieces with the seam allowance of your choice.

3 **Trim.** Use Pinking Shears to trim the excess or make notches on the curved seam allowances. Make a clip on both side gussets where the valley of the "V" shape is; do not cut the thread.

4 **Turn Right side out.** Turn the whole purse piece Right side out through the opening. Use your finger tip or something pointy (but not sharp) to round out the top curved seam.

5 **Press well.** Use an iron to press the purse piece well with a bit of steam to remove the wrinkles if necessary.

6 **Close the opening.** Use Ladder/Blind stitches to close the opening.

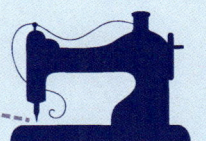

DIRECTIONS

Complete the Purse piece

7 **Top Stitch.** Top Stitch all the way around the top edge by using 1/16" seam allowance.

Do NOT use a seam allowance larger than 1/8", even though the top edge will be under the frame; using a seam allowance smaller than 1/8" will work well.

8 **Mark all 4 centers.** Press well if needed. Use chalk or erasable pen to mark all 4 centers.

Install the purse frame

1 **Install the purse frame.** Get the correct size and shape purse frame ready to install to the completed purse piece.

Please refer to the Chapter "Install Sew-In Purse Frame".

3.35" Round

3.35" Round

The Katy - *Faith*

3.35" (8.5 cm) Arch Purse Frame

II_R_V1

Front & Back

No Seam Allowance

1"

Printing Instructions

Please make sure your printer's scaling is set to "none," "actual size" or "100%". Do NOT check the "scale to fit paper size" option. Once the pattern is printed out, make sure it printed correctly. Check the "1 inch Square" and it should measure 1" x 1". If the square is not the correct size, check the printer settings again.

The Katy
Three pieces, Round shape frame

Iris

Hope

Grace

The Katy - Grace

3.35" (8.5 cm) Arch Purse Frame

III_R_V1

Front & Back

No Seam Allowance

1"

The Katy - Grace

3.35" (8.5 cm) Arch Purse Frame

III_R_V1

Side Gusset & Bottom

No Seam Allowance

Printing Instructions

Please make sure your printer's scaling is set to "none," "actual size" or "100%". Do NOT check the "scale to fit paper size" option. Once the pattern is printed out, make sure it printed correctly. Check the "1 inch Square" and it should measure 1" x 1". If the square is not the correct size, check the printer settings again.

Grace

The Katy - *Grace (III_R_V1)*

- **THREE-piece**
- **Round Shape Frame**
- **Variation 1**

Finished Size: (approximate measurements)

4.5" (Top W) x 1.5" (Bottom W)
3.5" (H) x 2" (D)

* Top W: the widest part; H: not including the frame;

NOTE:

*The attached pattern has **NO** seam allowances included. Refer to the Chapter "How to Use The Pattern" completely before cutting or sewing!* ☺

Fabric Cuts:

If you are using directional fabric, please make sure they are facing in the right direction.

Tips: *(1) Print 2 copies of the pattern or trace the pattern onto blank paper, (2) add seam allowances to your preference (1/4", 3/8" or 1/2") around one of the patterns, (3) transfer all the markings, (4) cut out the pattern without (Pattern A) and with (Pattern B) seam allowances.*

SEWING SKILL

★ *Beginner/Intermediate*

★★☆☆☆

DIFFICULT LEVEL

★ *Easy* ●●○○○

Main

Lining

Reference

★ *For cutting the **Directional fabrics** - please refer to the Chapter "**How to Use The Pattern**"*

★ *__Pattern A__ - the original pattern which has "**NO Seam Allowance**"*

★ *__Pattern B__ - the pattern which has the "**Seam Allowance**" of your choice (1/4", 3/8" or 1/2")*

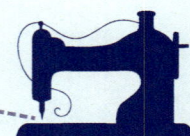

PREPARING ALL THE MATERIALS

✂ For NON-Directional Fabrics

Exterior/Interfacing:

- **Main** fabric - "Front & Back" (Pattern B) x 2; "Side Gusset & Bottom" (Pattern B) x 1;

- **Interfacing** - "Front & Back" (Pattern A) x 2; "Side Gusset & Bottom" (Pattern A) x 1; (no seam allowance needed)

Interior/Interfacing:

- **Lining** fabric - "Front & Back" (Pattern B) x 2; "Side Gusset & Bottom" (Pattern B) x 1;

- **Interfacing** - "Front & Back" (Pattern A) x 2; "Side Gusset & Bottom" (Pattern A) x 1; (no seam allowance needed)

✂ For Directional Fabrics

Exterior/Interfacing:

- **Main** fabric - "Front & Back": the same as non-directional fabrics;

- ✂ **"Side Gusset & Bottom":** Fold "Side Gusset & Bottom" (Pattern A) in half, add seam allowance all the way around (Pattern B) x 2;

- **Interfacing** - the same as above;

  *Tip: Do **NOT** apply the interfacing until the "Side Gusset & Bottom" pieces are connected together and become ONE piece.*

Interior/Interfacing: the same as above;

DIRECTIONS

For Directional Fabrics

The following steps are for those who will be using directional fabrics and/or making patchwork. If you are using non-directonal fabrics and don't want to make patchwork, you may skip these steps.

Prepare the Materials

1 **Cut the fabrics.** Please refer to the Chapter "How to Use The Pattern", under the Section "How to Modify the Pattern" - "1. Directional Fabric" and "3. Patchwork".

2 **Connect "Side Gusset & Bottom" together.** If you are using directional fabric on the "Side Gusset & Bottom" and/or making patchwork, you need more than one piece to connect them together. (Figure 1)

☞ If you cut the fabric in 2 pieces (fold in half at ①) - 2 x "Side Gusset & Bottom": Connect both pieces at the bottom edge, Right side facing together. Sew by using the seam allowance of your choice. (Figure 2)

☞ If you cut the fabric in 3 pieces (fold pattern at ②) - 2 x "Side Gusset" and 1 x "Bottom": Place the bottom of the "Side Gusset" and one of the longer edges of the "Bottom", Right side facing each other, and sew by using the seam allowance of your choice. (Figure 3)

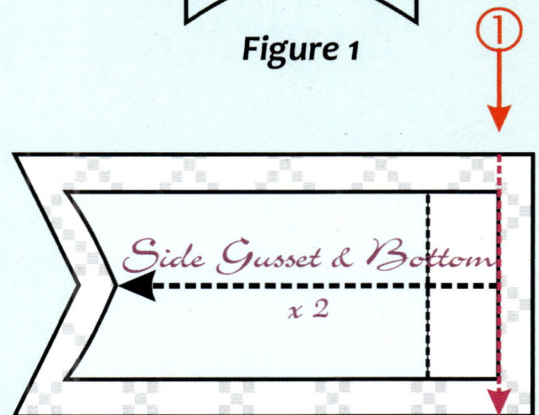

Figure 1

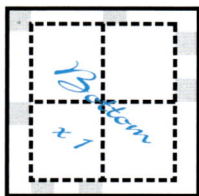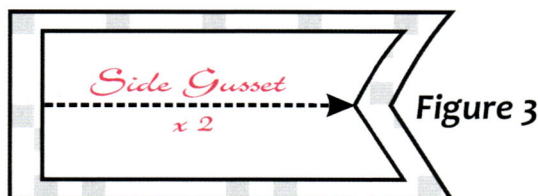

Figure 3

3 **Press the seam allowances open.** Press the seam allowances open at the Wrong side. Now, the "Side Gusset & Bottom" is ONE piece.

Figure 2

DIRECTIONS

Prepare the Materials

4 **Get the fabrics ready.** You should have three pieces of Main/Exterior, three pieces of Lining/Interior and all the interfacings ready.

5 **Fusing the fabrics.** Apply interfacing to the Wrong side of the main and lining fabrics, following the manufacturer's instructions. Please refer to the Section "Apply Interfacing" for more details.

*For those who use directional fabric and/or make patchwork, you may top stitch 1/8" or 1/16" away from the connecting edge **AFTER** applying the interfacing to the fabric.*

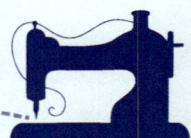

DIRECTIONS

Construct the Interior

1 **Trace Pattern A on the Wrong side.** Trace Pattern A (with NO seam allowance) to all the pieces on the Wrong side of the fabrics and transfer all the markings as well.

2 **Align Center.** Place one of the "Front & Back" pieces, Right side up, under the "Side Gusset & Bottom", Wrong side up. Align both centers, the bottom center of the "Front & Back" and the middle of the "Side Gusset & Bottom".

Use pins or clips to hold them in place. Make sure all the markings are aligned.

3 **Snip.** Snip within the seam allowance on the "Side Gusset & Bottom" piece, which has a straight seam. This makes it easier to line up with the curved seam on the "Front & Back" piece.

4 **Pin or clip all the way around.** Align all the markings.

② **Center Alignment**

①

"Side Gusset & Bottom"

"Front & Back"

DIRECTIONS

Construct the Interior

5 Sew all the way around. Sew all the way around by using the seam allowance of your choice. Start from marking ①, leave an opening, and end at marking ②.

SLOW DOWN while sewing on the curved seam. Please refer to the Chapter "Sewing the Curved Seam".

LEAVE AN OPENING at the bottom along the straight steam to turn the whole piece Right side out later.

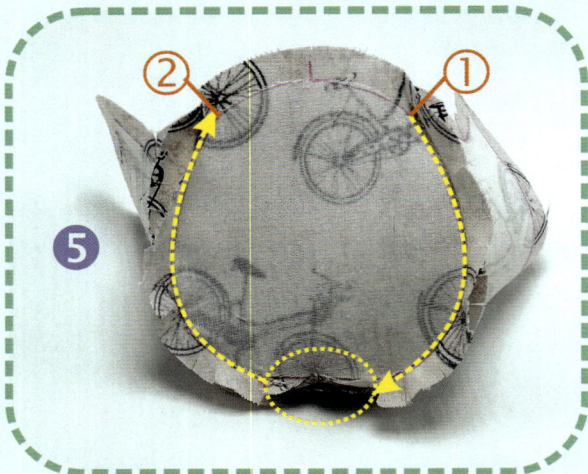

6 Repeat steps 2 to 5 on the other side. Repeat the same steps on the other side, but do NOT leave an opening, unless you forgot the first time.

Leave an opening on one side at the bottom straight seam

DIRECTIONS

Construct the Interior

7 **Press seam allowances open and Make notches.** Press the seam allowances open and trim the excess; make notches at the curved seam allowances, do not cut the threads. Now, the Lining piece is ready, let's put it aside.

Construct the Exterior

1 **Construct the exterior** using the same process as you did with the lining, except you do NOT need to leave an opening. Sew the exterior by using the seam allowance of your choice.

✎ **NO** need to leave an opening. **SEW SLOWLY** on the curved seam.

Completed Interior

Completed Exterior

DIRECTIONS

Complete the Purse piece

1 **Get both Main and Lining pieces ready to connect.** You should have both Main and Lining pieces ready to complete the purse piece. Place the Main piece (Right side out) into the Lining piece (Wrong side out), with the Right sides of both pieces facing each other. Align all 4 center markings.

*Use chalk or erasable pen to draw the seam line on the Wrong side of the Lining **before** sewing.*

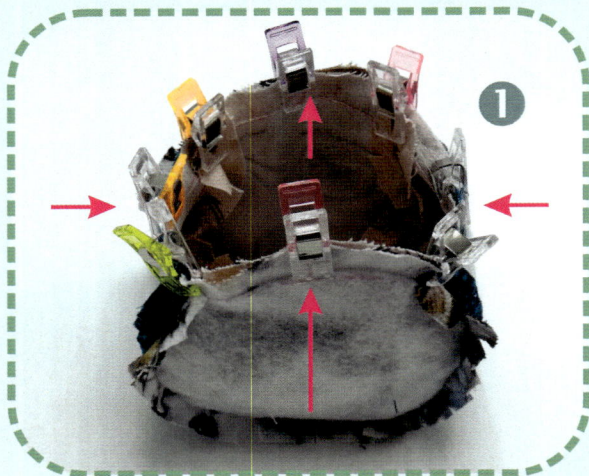

2 **Sew all the way around.** Sew all the way around the top edge to connect both pieces by using the seam allowance of your choice.

3 **Trim.** Use Pinking Shears to trim the excess or make notches on the curved seam allowances. Make a clip on both side gussets where the valley of the "V" shape is; do not cut the thread.

4 **Turn Right side out.** Turn the whole purse piece Right side out through the opening. Use your finger tip or something pointy (but not sharp) to round out the top curved seam.

5 **Press well.** Use an iron to press the purse piece with a bit of steam to remove wrinkles if necessary.

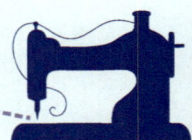

Complete the Purse piece

6 **Close the opening.** Use Ladder/Blind stitches to close the opening.

7 **Top Stitch.** Top Stitch all the way around the top edge by using 1/16" seam allowance.

Do NOT use a seam allowance larger than 1/8", even though the top edge will be under the frame; using a seam allowance smaller than 1/8" will work well.

8 **Mark all 4 centers.** Press well if needed. Use chalk or erasable pen to mark all 4 centers.

Install the purse frame

1 **Install the purse frame.** Get the correct size and shape purse frame ready to install to the completed purse piece.

Please refer to the Chapter "Install Sew-In Purse Frame".

3.35" Round

3.35" Round

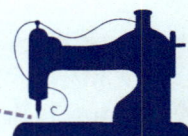

** *Please refer to the pattern, "Grace", for instructions on how to construct this pattern.* **

Hope

The Katy - Hope (III_R_V2)

- **THREE-piece**
- **Round Shape Frame**
- **Variation 2**

Finished Size: (approximate measurements)

4" (Top W) x 2.5" (Bottom W)
3.5" (H) x 2" (D)

* Top W: the widest part; H: not including the frame;

NOTE:

*The attached pattern has **NO** seam allowances included. Refer to the Chapter "How to Use The Pattern" completely before cutting or sewing!* ☺

Fabric Cuts:

If you are using directional fabric, please make sure they are facing in the right direction.

Tips: *(1) Print 2 copies of the pattern or trace the pattern onto blank paper, (2) add seam allowances to your preference (1/4", 3/8" or 1/2") around one of the patterns, (3) transfer all the markings, (4) cut out the pattern without (Pattern A) and with (Pattern B) seam allowances.*

SEWING SKILL

★ Beginner/Intermediate

★★☆☆☆

DIFFICULT LEVEL

★ Easy ●●○○○

The Katy - Hope
3.35" (8.5 cm) Arch Purse Frame

III_R_V2

Front & Back

No Seam Allowance

1"

The Katy - Hope
3.35" (8.5 cm) Arch Purse Frame

III_R_V2

Side Gusset & Bottom

No Seam Allowance

Printing Instructions

*P*lease make sure your printer's scaling is set to "none," "actual size" or "100%". Do NOT check the "scale to fit paper size" option. Once the pattern is printed out, make sure it printed correctly. Check the "1 inch Square" and it should measure 1" x 1". If the square is not the correct size, check the printer settings again.

The Katy - Iris

3.35" (8.5 cm) Arch Purse Frame

III_R_V3

Side Gusset

No Seam Allowance

1"

The Katy - Iris

3.35" (8.5 cm) Arch Purse Frame

III_R_V3

Front & Back

No Seam Allowance

Printing Instructions

Please make sure your printer's scaling is set to "none," "actual size" or "100%". Do NOT check the "scale to fit paper size" option. Once the pattern is printed out, make sure it printed correctly. Check the "1 inch Square" and it should measure 1" x 1". If the square is not the correct size, check the printer settings again.

Iris

The Katy - Iris (III_R_V3)

- **THREE-piece**
- **Round Shape Frame**
- **Variation 3**

Finished Size: (approximate measurements)

4.25" (Top W) x 3" (Bottom W)
3.5" (H) x 2.25" (D)

* Top W: the widest part; H: not including the frame;

NOTE:

*The attached pattern has **NO** seam allowances included. Refer to the Chapter "How to Use The Pattern" completely before cutting or sewing!* ☺

Fabric Cuts:

If you are using directional fabric, please make sure they are facing in the right direction.

Tips: *(1) Print 2 copies of the pattern or trace the pattern onto blank paper, (2) add seam allowances to your preference (1/4", 3/8" or 1/2") around one of the patterns, (3) transfer all the markings, (4) cut out the pattern without (Pattern A) and with (Pattern B) seam allowances.*

SEWING SKILL

★ Beginner/Intermediate

★★☆☆☆

DIFFICULT LEVEL

★ Easy ●●○○○

PREPARATION

** This is not an actual size.**
Please use the pattern on page 101.

Add seam allowance cut 1

The Katy - Iris
3.35" (8.5 cm) Arch Purse Frame
III_R_V3
Front & Back
No Seam Allowance

The Katy - Iris
3.35" (8.5 cm) Arch Purse Frame
III_R_V3
Side Gusset
No Seam Allowance

Add seam allowance cut 2

Reference

★ *For cutting the **Directional fabrics** - please refer to the Chapter "**How to Use The Pattern**"*

★ *__Pattern A__ - the original pattern which has "**NO Seam Allowance**"*

★ *__Pattern B__ - the pattern which has the "**Seam Allowance**" of your choice (1/4", 3/8" or 1/2")*

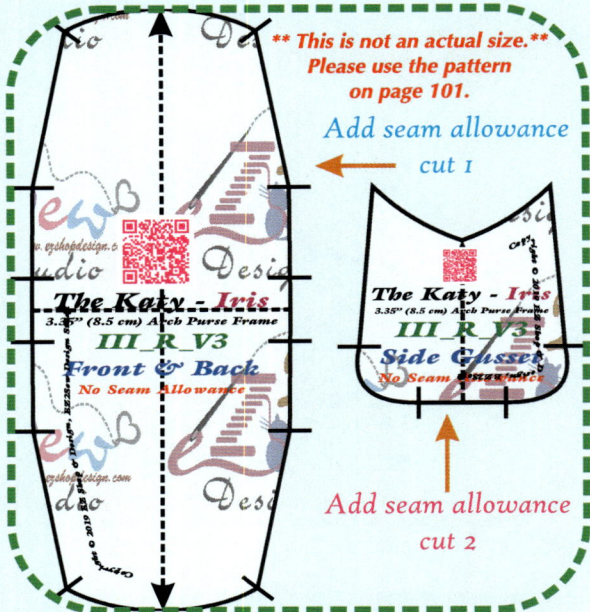

PREPARING ALL THE MATERIALS

✄ For NON-Directional Fabrics

Exterior/Interfacing:

- **Main** fabric - "Front & Back" (Pattern B) x 1; "Side Gusset" (Pattern B) x 2;

- **Interfacing** - "Front & Back" (Pattern A) x 1; "Side Gusset" (Pattern A) x 2; (no seam allowance needed)

Interior/Interfacing:

- **Lining** fabric - "Front & Back" (Pattern B) x 1; "Side Gusset" (Pattern B) x 2;

- **Interfacing** - "Front & Back" (Pattern A) x 1; "Side Gusset" (Pattern A) x 2; (no seam allowance needed)

✄ For Directional Fabrics

Exterior/Interfacing:

- **Main** fabric - "Side Gusset": the same as non-directional fabrics;

- ✄ **"Front & Back":** Fold "Front & Back" (Pattern A) in half, add seam allowance all the way around (Pattern B) x 2;

- **Interfacing** - the same as above;

*Tip: Do **NOT** apply the interfacing until the "Front & Back" pieces are connected together and become ONE piece.*

Interior/Interfacing: the same as above;

DIRECTIONS

For Directional Fabrics

The following steps are for those who will be using directional fabrics and/or making patchwork. If you are using non-directonal fabrics and don't want to make patchwork, you may skip these steps.

Prepare the Materials

1 **Cut the fabrics.** Please refer to the Chapter "How to Use The Pattern", under the Section "How to Modify the Pattern" - "1. Directional Fabric" and "3. Patchwork".

2 **Connect "Front & Back" together.** If you are using directional fabric on the "Front & Back" and/or making patchwork, you need more than one piece to connect them together. (Figure 1)

☞ If you cut the fabric in 2 pieces (fold in half at ①) - 2 x "Front & Back": Connect both pieces at the bottom edge, Right sides facing together. Sew by using the seam allowance of your choice. (Figure 2)

☞ If you cut the fabric in 3 pieces (fold pattern at ②) - 1 x "Front", 1 x "Back" and 1 x "Bottom": Place the bottom of the "Front" (or "Back") and one of the shorter edges of the "Bottom", Right side facing each other, and sew by using the seam allowance of your choice. Repeat the same step on the other side.

Figure 3

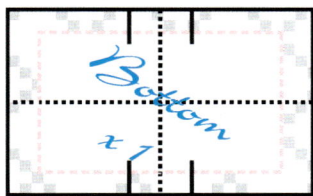

3 **Press the seam allowances open.** Press the seam allowances open at the Wrong side. Now, the "Front & Back" is ONE piece.

Figure 1

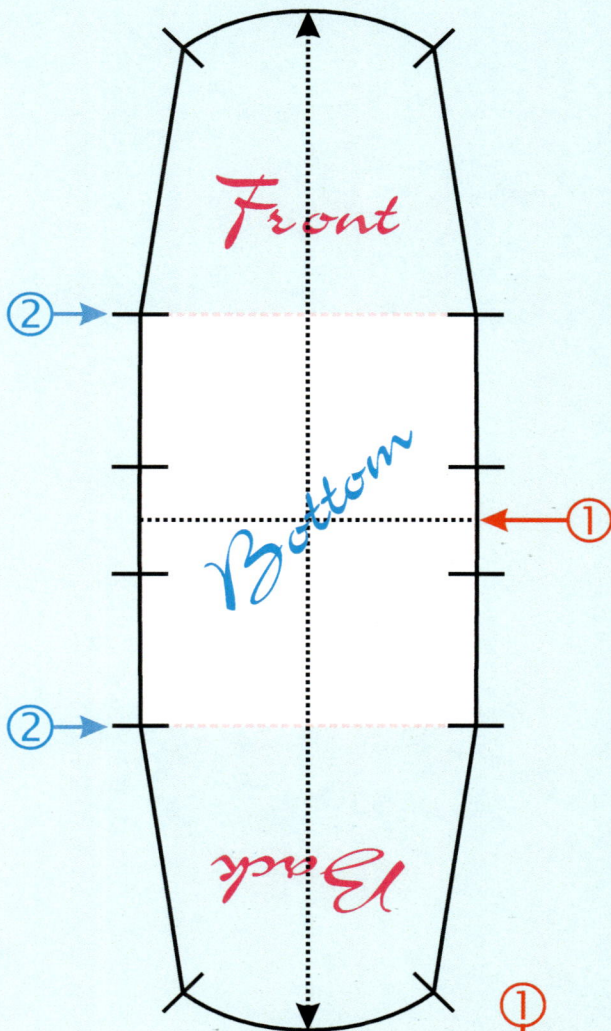

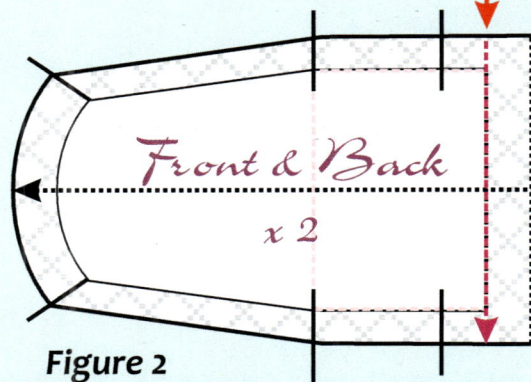

Figure 2

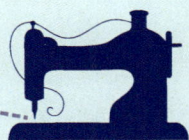

DIRECTIONS

Front ① Back

Bottom

② Bottom

③

Press the seam allowances open

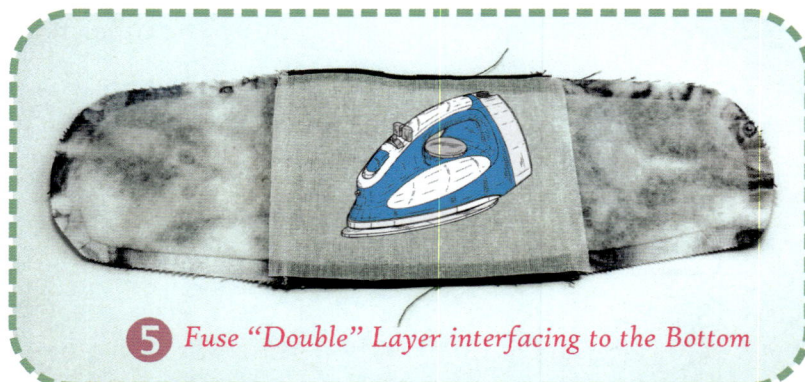

Prepare the Materials

4 **Get the fabrics ready.** You should have three pieces of Main/Exterior, three pieces of Lining/Interior and all the interfacings ready.

5 **Fusing the fabrics.** Apply interfacing to the Wrong side of the main and lining fabrics, following the manufacturer's instructions. Please refer to the Section "Apply Interfacing" for more details.

*For those who use directional fabric and/or make patchwork, you may top stitch 1/8" or 1/16" away from the connecting edge **AFTER** applying the interfacing to the fabric.*

④ Main/Exterior   ⑤ Top Stitch

⑤ Fuse "Double" Layer interfacing to the Bottom

DIRECTIONS

Construct the Interior

1 **Trace Pattern A on the Wrong side.** Trace Pattern A (with NO seam allowance) to all the pieces on the Wrong side of the fabrics and transfer all the markings as well.

2 **Align Center.** Place one of the "Side Gusset" pieces, Right side up, under the "Front & Back", Wrong side up. Align the centers of both the bottom "Side Gusset" and the middle of the "Front & Back" piece.

✍ Use pins or clips to hold them in place. Make sure all the markings are aligned.

3 **Snip.** Snip within the seam allowance on the "Front & Back" piece, which has a straight seam. This makes it easier to line up with the curved seam on the "Side Gusset".

4 **Pin or clip all the way around.** Align all the markings.

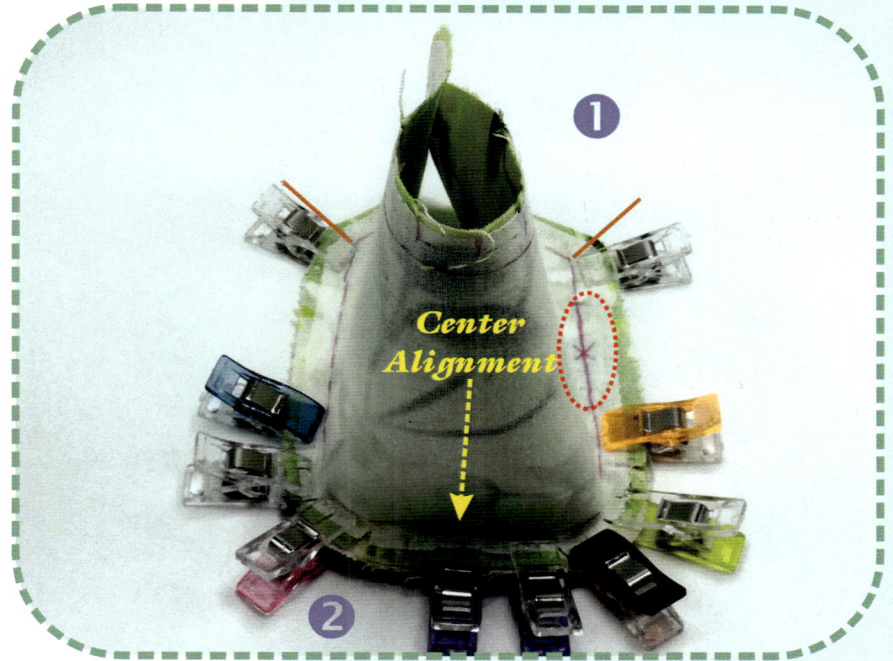

DIRECTIONS

Construct the Interior

5 **Sew all the way around.** Sew all the way around by using the seam allowance of your choice. Start from marking ①, leave an opening, and end at marking ②.

✎ **SLOW DOWN** *while sewing on the curved seam. Please refer to the Chapter "Sewing the Curved Seam".*

✎ **LEAVE AN OPENING** *at the side or bottom along the straight steam to turn the whole piece Right side out later.*

6 **Repeat steps 2 to 5 on the other side.** Repeat the same steps on the other side, but do NOT leave an opening, unless you forgot the first time.

Leave an opening at the straight seam

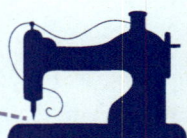

DIRECTIONS

Construct the Interior

7 **Press seam allowances open and Make notches.** Press the seam allowances open and trim the excess; make notches at the curved seam allowances, do not cut the threads. Now, the Lining piece is ready, let's put it aside.

Construct the Exterior

1 **Construct the exterior** using the same process as you did with the lining, except you do NOT need to leave an opening. Sew the exterior by using the seam allowance of your choice.

✍ *NO need to leave an opening.* ***SEW SLOWLY*** *on the curved seam.*

DIRECTIONS

Complete the Purse piece

Completed Interior ❶

Completed Exterior

1 **Get both Main and Lining pieces ready to connect.** You should have both Main and Lining pieces ready to complete the purse piece. Place the Main piece (Right side out) into the Lining piece (Wrong side out), with the Right sides of both pieces facing each other. Align all 4 center markings.

*Use chalk or erasable pen to draw the seam line on the Wrong side of the Lining **before** sewing.*

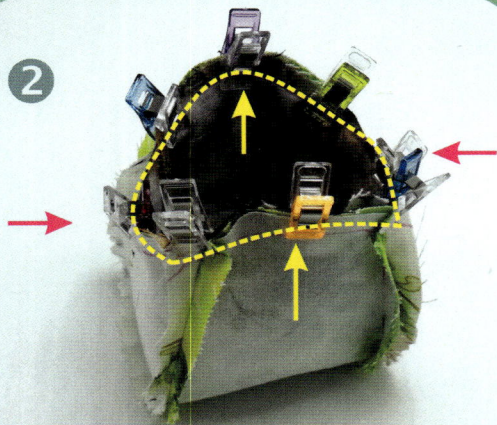

❷

2 **Sew all the way around.** Sew all the way around the top edge to connect both pieces by using the seam allowance of your choice.

3 **Trim.** Use Pinking Shears to trim the excess or make notches on the curved seam allowances. Make a clip on both side gussets where the valley of the "V" shape is; do not cut the thread.

4 **Turn Right side out.** Turn the whole purse piece Right side out through the opening. Use your finger tip or something pointy (but not sharp) to round out the top curved seam.

❸

5 **Press well.** Use an iron to press the purse piece with a bit of steam to remove wrinkles if necessary.

❺

Complete the Purse piece

6 **Close the opening.** Use Ladder/Blind stitches to close the opening.

7 **Top Stitch.** Top Stitch all the way around the top edge by using 1/16" seam allowance.

Do NOT use a seam allowance larger than 1/8", even though the top edge will be under the frame; using a seam allowance smaller than 1/8" will work well.

8 **Mark all 4 centers.** Press well if needed. Use chalk or erasable pen to mark all 4 centers.

Install the purse frame

1 **Install the purse frame.** Get the correct size and shape purse frame ready to install to the completed purse piece.

Please refer to the Chapter "Install Sew-In Purse Frame".

3.35" Round

The Katy

Four pieces, *Round* shape frame

Jade

Kaylee

The Katy - Jade
3.35" (8.5 cm) Arch Purse Frame
IV_R_VI
Front & Back
No Seam Allowance

The Katy - Jade
3.35" (8.5 cm) Arch Purse Frame
IV_R_VI
Side Gusset
No Seam Allowance

1"

Printing Instructions

Please make sure your printer's scaling is set to "none," "actual size" or "100%". Do NOT check the "scale to fit paper size" option. Once the pattern is printed out, make sure it printed correctly. Check the "1 inch Square" and it should measure 1" x 1". If the square is not the correct size, check the printer settings again.

The Katy - Kaylee
3.35" (8.5 cm) Arch Purse Frame
IV_R_V2
Front & Back
No Seam Allowance

The Katy - Kaylee
3.35" (8.5 cm) Arch Purse Frame
IV_R_V2
Side Gusset
No Seam Allowance

113

Jade

The Katy - Jade (IV_R_V1)

- **FOUR-piece**
- **Round Shape Frame**
- **Variation 1**

Finished Size: (approximate measurements)

4" (Top W) x 2.25" (Bottom W)
3.25" (H) x 2.25" (D)

* Top W: the widest part; H: not including the frame;

NOTE:

*The attached pattern has **NO** seam allowances included. Refer to the Chapter "How to Use The Pattern" completely before cutting or sewing!* ☺

Fabric Cuts:

If you are using directional fabric, please make sure they are facing in the right direction.

Tips: *(1) Print 2 copies of the pattern or trace the pattern onto blank paper, (2) add seam allowances to your preference (1/4", 3/8" or 1/2") around one of the patterns, (3) transfer all the markings, (4) cut out the pattern without (Pattern A) and with (Pattern B) seam allowances.*

SEWING SKILL

★ Beginner/Intermediate

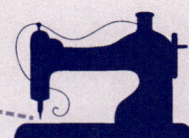

★★☆☆☆

DIFFICULT LEVEL

★ Intermediate ●●●○○

PREPARATION

Main

Lining

PREPARING ALL THE MATERIALS

✂ **For NON-Directional Fabrics**

Exterior/Interfacing:

- **Main** fabric - "Front & Back" (Pattern B) x 2; "Side Gusset" (Pattern B) x 2;

- **Interfacing** - "Front & Back" (Pattern A) x 2; "Side Gusset" (Pattern A) x 2; (no seam allowance needed)

Interior/Interfacing:

- **Lining** fabric - "Front & Back" (Pattern B) x 2; "Side Gusset" (Pattern B) x 2;

- **Interfacing** - "Front & Back" (Pattern A) x 2; "Side Gusset" (Pattern A) x 2; (no seam allowance needed)

✂ **For Directional Fabrics**

Exterior/Interfacing:

- **Main** fabric - the same as non-directional fabrics;

- **Interfacing** - the same as above;

Interior/Interfacing:

- **Main** fabric - the same as non-directional fabrics;

- **Interfacing** - the same as above;

*P*lease refer to the Section "Apply Interfacing" for more details on how to "Apply Single or Double Layer" interfacing.

Reference

★ For cutting the **Directional fabrics** - please refer to the Chapter "**How to Use The Pattern**"

★ **Pattern A** - the original pattern which has "**NO Seam Allowance**"

★ **Pattern B** - the pattern which has the "**Seam Allowance**" of your choice (1/4", 3/8" or 1/2")

DIRECTIONS

For Directional Fabrics

There is no difference between cutting directional and non-directional fabrics for this 4-piece pattern. If you are using directional fabrics, make sure they are in the correct direction.

Prepare the Materials

1 **Cut the fabrics and interfacing.** You should have 4 pieces of Main/Exterior (2 x "Front & Back" and 2 x "Side Gusset"), 4 pieces of Lining/Interior (2 x "front & Back" and 2 x "Side Gusset") and all the interfacings ready.

2 **Fusing the fabrics.** Apply interfacing to the Wrong side of the main and lining fabrics, following the manufacturer's instructions. Please refer to the Section "Apply Interfacing" for more details.

①

②

Lining

Main

Double Layer Interfacing

Note

*I*f you would like a more structured look, you might want to apply two layers of interfacing (check "Exhibit 1" photos). If you would like a softer feel, then a single layer of fleece will work (check "Exhibit 2" photos).

DIRECTIONS

Construct the Interior

1 **Trace Pattern A on the Wrong side of the fabrics.** Trace Pattern A (with NO seam allowance) to all the pieces on the Wrong side of the fabric and transfer all the markings as well.

2 **Align Markings.** Place one of the "Front & Back" pieces, Right side up, under one of the "Side Gusset" pieces, Wrong side up. Align both bottom-centers at marking ②, and marking ①. Repeat the same step on the other "Front & Back" and "Side Gusset".

Note

*T*his is one of my favorite patterns. It's not very difficult to sew, but it requires some time to trace all the patterns and align all the markings before you sew. It really pays off to focus on the details more. Hope you will enjoy it! ☺

Use pins or clips to hold them in place. Make sure all the markings are aligned.

3 **Sew.** Start from ① and stop at ② by using the seam allowance of your choice on both pairs of "Front & Back" and "Side Gusset".

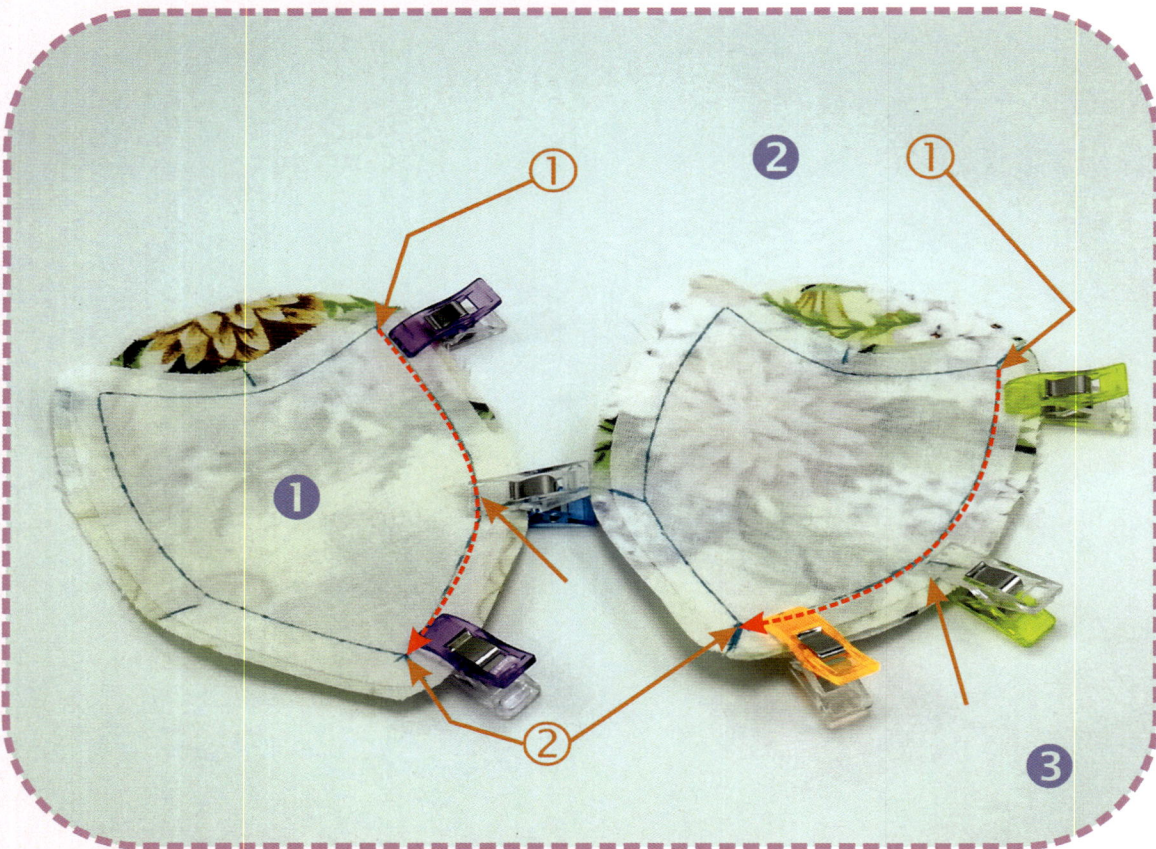

DIRECTIONS

Construct the Interior

4 **Connect.** Now, you should have two pairs of connected "Front & Back" and "Side Gusset" pieces. Press the seam allowances open. Place both pieces Right side facing each other, align all the markings, especially the center seam at the bottom of both pieces.

Make sure all the markings are aligned, especially the center connected seam. If both center seams did not align well, the bottom will look crooked.

5 **Sew all the way around.** Sew all the way around by using the seam allowance of your choice. Start from marking ①, leave an opening, and end at marking ②.

SLOW DOWN while sewing on the curved seam. Please refer to the Chapter "Sewing the Curved Seam".

*LEAVE AN OPENING at the side that has the **straight** seam for turning the whole piece Right side out later.*

6 **Make notches and Press well.** Cut notches or clips at all the curved seams. Press all the seam allowances open, trim the excess if necessary. Put aside the completed Lining piece.

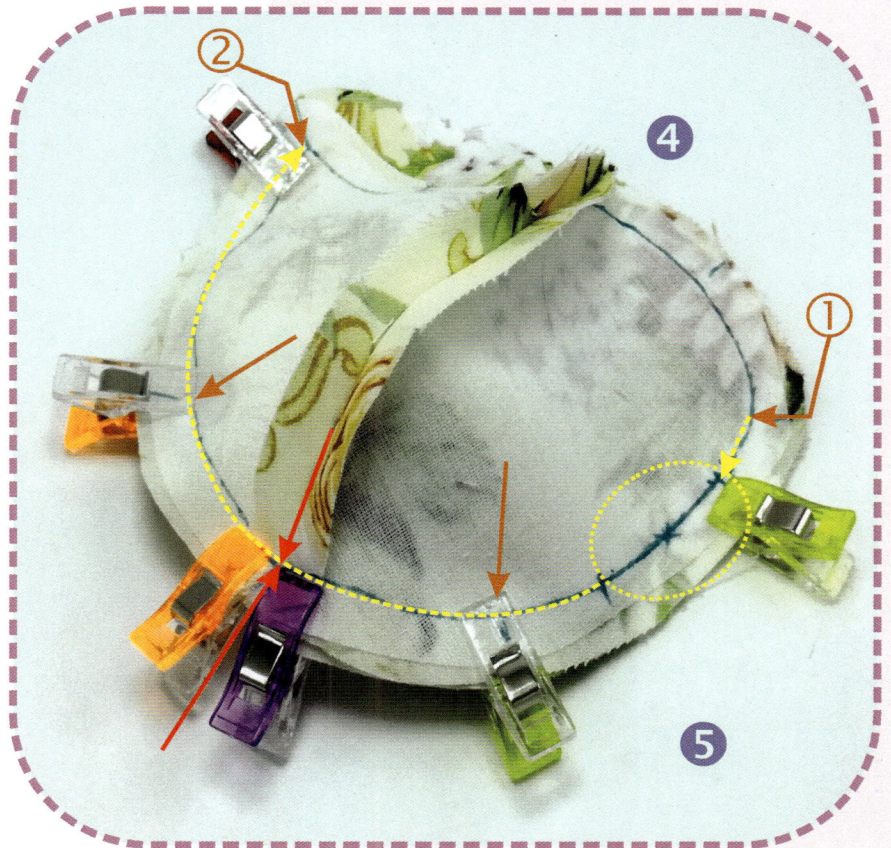

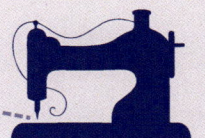

DIRECTIONS

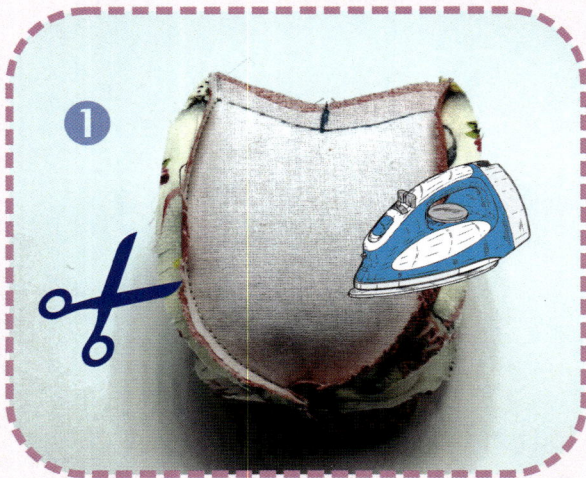

Construct the Exterior

1 **Construct the exterior** using the same process as you did with the lining, except you do NOT need to leave an opening. Sew the exterior by using the seam allowance of your choice.

*NO need to leave an opening. **SEW SLOWLY** on the curved seam.*

Complete the Purse piece

1 **Get both Main and Lining pieces ready to connect.** You should have both Main and Lining pieces ready to complete the purse piece. Place the Main piece (Right side out) into the Lining piece (Wrong side out), with the Right sides of both pieces facing each other. Align all 4 center markings.

*Use chalk or erasable pen to draw the seam line on the Wrong side of the Lining **before** sewing.*

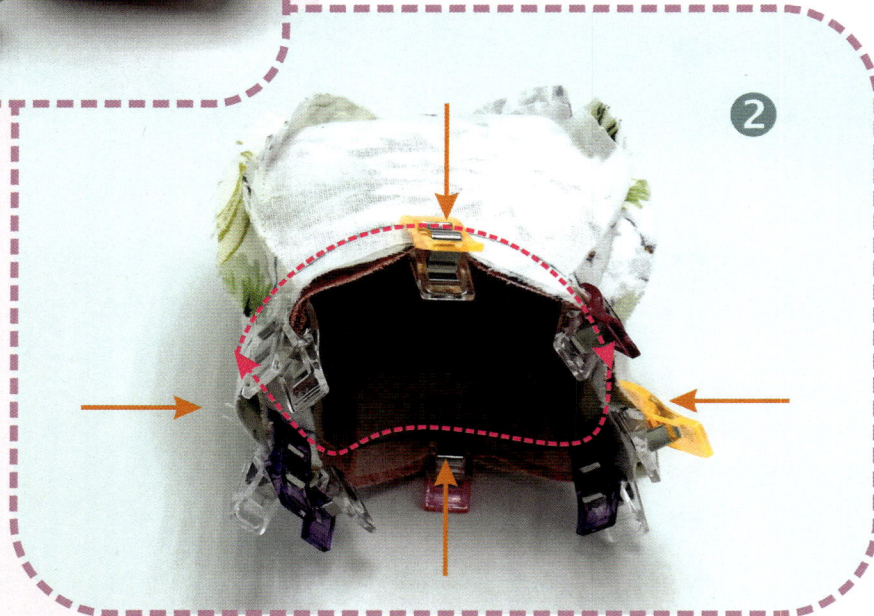

2 **Sew all the way around.** Sew all the way around the top edge to connect both pieces with the seam allowance of your choice.

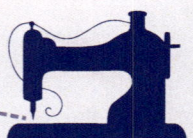

DIRECTIONS

Complete the Purse piece

3 **Trim.** Use Pinking Shears to trim the excess or make notches at the curved seam allowances. Make a clip on both side gussets where the valley of the "V" shape is; do not cut the thread.

4 **Turn Right side out.** Turn the whole purse piece Right side out through the opening. Use your finger tip or something pointy (but not sharp) to round out the top curved seam.

5 **Press well.** Use an iron to press the purse piece well with a bit of steam to remove the wrinkles if necessary.

6 **Close the opening.** Use Ladder/Blind stitches to close the opening.

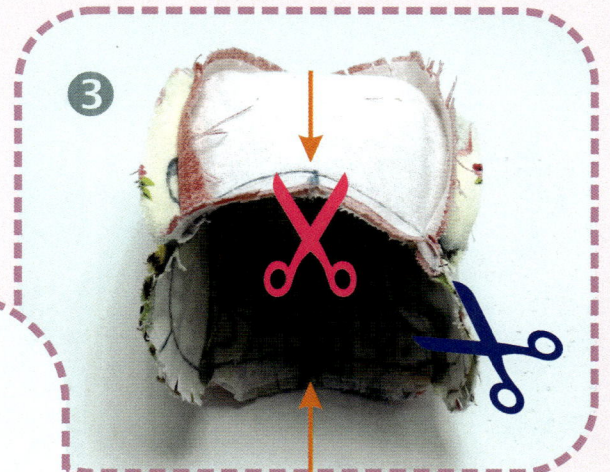

③

③

⑥

Note

*P*lease refer to the Chapter "Basic Stitches" for more details on how to close the opening.

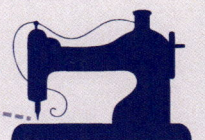

Complete the Purse piece

7 **Top Stitch.** Top Stitch all the way around the top edge by using 1/16" seam allowance.

✍ *Do NOT use a seam allowance larger than 1/8", even though the top edge will be under the frame; using a seam allowance smaller than 1/8" will work well.*

8 **Mark all 4 centers.** Press well if needed. Use chalk or erasable pen to mark all 4 centers.

Install the purse frame

1 **Install the purse frame.** Get the correct size and shape purse frame ready to install to the completed purse piece.

✍ *Please refer to the Chapter "Install Sew-In Purse Frame".*

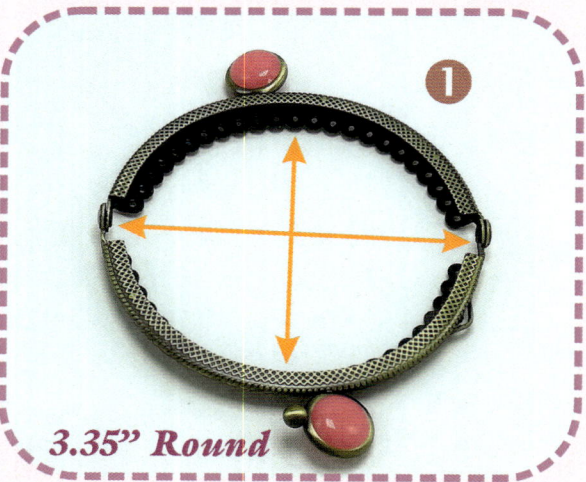

3.35" Round

3.35" Round

EXHIBIT 1

EXHIBIT 2

** Please refer to the pattern, "Jade", for instructions on how to construct this pattern. **

Kaylee

The Katy - Kaylee (IV_R_V2)

- **FOUR**-piece
- **Round Shape Frame**
- **Variation 2**

Finished Size: (approximate measurements)

4" (Top W) x 2.5" (Bottom W)
3.5" (H) x 2.5" (D)

* Top W: the widest part; H: not including the frame;

NOTE:

The attached pattern has **NO** seam allowances included. Refer to the Chapter "How to Use The Pattern" completely before cutting or sewing! ☺

Fabric Cuts:

If you are using directional fabric, please make sure they are facing in the right direction.

Tips: (1) Print 2 copies of the pattern or trace the pattern onto blank paper, (2) add seam allowances to your preference (1/4", 3/8" or 1/2") around one of the patterns, (3) transfer all the markings, (4) cut out the pattern without (Pattern A) and with (Pattern B) seam allowances.

This photo was borrowed from the pattern The Katy - "Hope".

SEWING SKILL

★ Beginner/Intermediate

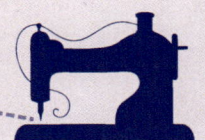

★★☆☆☆

DIFFICULT LEVEL

★ Intermediate ●●●○○

The Katy

Four pieces, Oval shape frame

Mila

Lauren

The Katy - Lauren
3.35" (8.5 cm) Arch Purse Frame
IV_0_V1
Front & Back
No Seam Allowance

The Katy - Lauren
3.35" (8.5 cm) Arch Purse Frame
IV_0_V1
Side Gusset
No Seam Allowance

1"

Printing Instructions

*P*lease make sure your printer's scaling is set to "none," "actual size" or "100%". Do NOT check the "scale to fit paper size" option. Once the pattern is printed out, make sure it printed correctly. Check the "1 inch Square" and it should measure 1" x 1". If the square is not the correct size, check the printer settings again.

The Katy - Mila
3.35" (8.5 cm) Arch Purse Frame
IV_0_V2
Front & Back
No Seam Allowance

The Katy - Mila
3.35" (8.5 cm) Arch Purse Frame
IV_0_V2
Side Gusset
No Seam Allowance

Lauren

The Katy - Lauren (IV_O_V1)

- **FOUR-piece**
- **Oval Shape Frame**
- **Variation 1**

Finished Size: (approximate measurements)

4" (Top W) x 2.25" (Bottom W)
3.25" (H) x 2.5" (D)

* Top W: the widest part; H: not including the frame;

NOTE:

*The attached pattern has **NO** seam allowances included. Refer to the Chapter "How to Use The Pattern" completely before cutting or sewing!* ☺

Fabric Cuts:

If you are using directional fabric, please make sure they are facing in the right direction.

Tips: *(1) Print 2 copies of the pattern or trace the pattern onto blank paper, (2) add seam allowances to your preference (1/4", 3/8" or 1/2") around one of the patterns, (3) transfer all the markings, (4) cut out the pattern without (Pattern A) and with (Pattern B) seam allowances.*

SEWING SKILL

★ Beginner/Intermediate

★★☆☆☆

DIFFICULT LEVEL

★ Intermediate ●●●○○

PREPARATION

Lining *Main*

Interfacing

Reference

★ *For cutting the* **Directional fabrics** - *please refer to the Chapter* **"How to Use The Pattern"**

★ **Pattern A** - *the original pattern which has* **"NO Seam Allowance"**

★ **Pattern B** - *the pattern which has the* **"Seam Allowance"** *of your choice (1/4", 3/8" or 1/2")*

PREPARING ALL THE MATERIALS

✂ For NON-Directional Fabrics

Exterior/Interfacing:

- **Main** fabric - "Front & Back" (Pattern B) x 2; "Side Gusset" (Pattern B) x 2;

- **Interfacing** - "Front & Back" (Pattern A) x 2; "Side Gusset" (Pattern A) x 2; (no seam allowance needed)

Interior/Interfacing:

- **Lining** fabric - "Front & Back" (Pattern B) x 2; "Side Gusset" (Pattern B) x 2;

- **Interfacing** - "Front & Back" (Pattern A) x 2; "Side Gusset" (Pattern A) x 2; (no seam allowance needed)

✂ For Directional Fabrics

Exterior/Interfacing:

- **Main** fabric - the same as non-directional fabrics;

- **Interfacing** - the same as above;

Interior/Interfacing:

- **Main** fabric - the same as non-directional fabrics;

- **Interfacing** - the same as above;

 *P*lease refer to the Section "Apply Interfacing" for more details on how to "Apply Single or Double Layer" interfacing.

DIRECTIONS

For Directional Fabrics

There is no difference between cutting directional and non-directional fabrics for this 4-piece pattern. If you are using directional fabrics, make sure they are in the correct direction.

Prepare the Materials

1 **Cut the fabrics and interfacing.** You should have 4 pieces of Main/Exterior (2 x "Front & Back" and 2 x "Side Gusset"), 4 pieces of Lining/Interior (2 x "front & Back" and 2 x "Side Gusset") and all the interfacings ready.

2 **Fusing the fabrics.** Apply interfacing to the Wrong side of the main and lining fabrics, following the manufacturer's instructions. Please refer to the Section "Apply Interfacing" for more details.

Lining Main

Interfacing

①

Main

Double Layer Interfacing

Lining

②

Note

If you would like a more structured look, you might want to apply two layers of interfacing. If you would like a softer feel, then a single layer of fleece will work.

DIRECTIONS

Construct the Interior

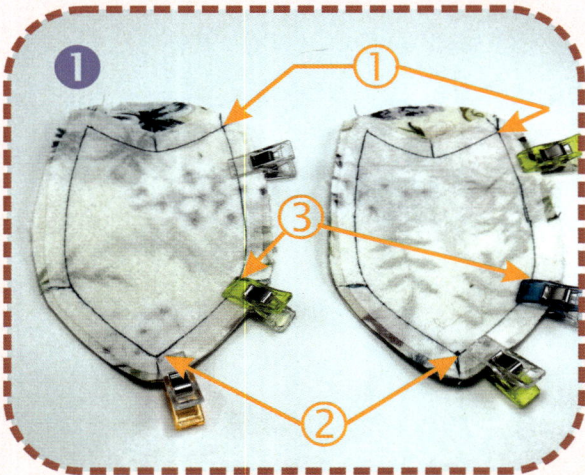

1 **Trace Pattern A on the Wrong side of the fabrics.** Trace Pattern A (with NO seam allowance) to all the pieces on the Wrong side of the fabric and transfer all the markings as well.

2 **Align Markings.** Place one of the "Front & Back" pieces, Right side up, under one of the "Side Gusset" pieces, Wrong side up. Align both bottom-centers at marking ②, and marking ①. Repeat the same step on the other "Front & Back" and "Side Gusset".

Use pins or clips to hold them in place. Make sure all the markings are aligned.

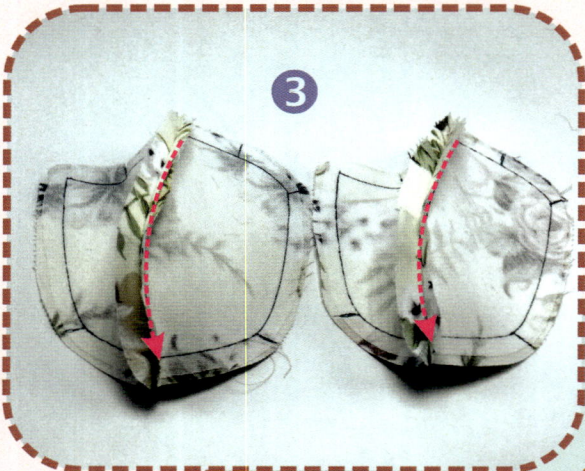

3 **Sew.** Start from ① and stop at ② by using the seam allowance of your choice on both pairs of "Front & Back" and "Side Gusset".

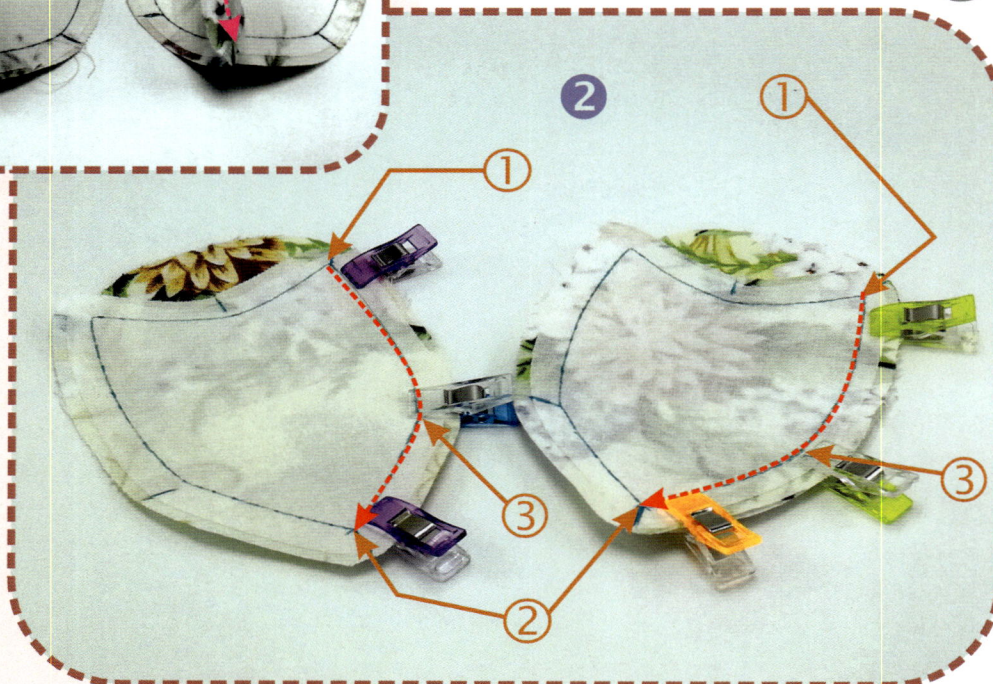

Construct the Interior

4 **Connect.** Now, you should have two pairs of connected "Front & Back" and "Side Gusset" pieces. Press the seam allowances open. Place both pieces Right side facing each other, align all the markings, especially the center seam at the bottom of both pieces.

Make sure all the markings are aligned, especially the center connected seam. If both center seams did not align well, the bottom will look crooked.

5 **Sew all the way around.** Sew all the way around by using the seam allowance of your choice. Start from marking ①, leave an opening, and end at marking ②.

SLOW DOWN while sewing on the curved seam. Please refer to the Chapter "Sewing the Curved Seam".

*LEAVE AN OPENING at the side that has the **straight** seam for turning the whole piece Right side out later.*

6 **Make notches and Press well.** Cut notches or clips at all the curved seams. Press all the seam allowances open, trim the excess if necessary. Put aside the completed Lining piece.

DIRECTIONS

Construct the Exterior

1 **Construct the exterior** using the same process as you did with the lining, except you do NOT need to leave an opening. Sew the exterior by using the seam allowance of your choice.

✍ *NO need to leave an opening.* **SEW SLOWLY** *on the curved seam.*

Complete the Purse piece

1 **Get both Main and Lining pieces ready to connect.** You should have both Main and Lining pieces ready to complete the purse piece. Place the Main piece (Right side out) into the Lining piece (Wrong side out), with the Right sides of both pieces facing each other. Align all 4 center markings.

✍ *Use chalk or erasable pen to draw the seam line on the Wrong side of the Lining* **before** *sewing.*

2 **Sew all the way around.** Sew all the way around the top edge to connect both pieces with the seam allowance of your choice.

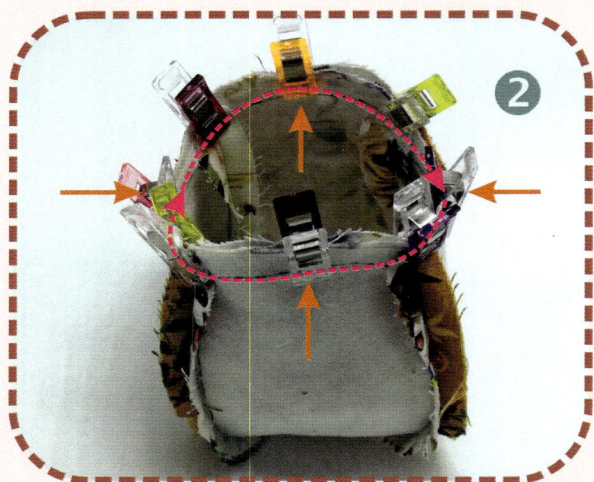

Complete the Purse piece

3 **Trim.** Use Pinking Shears to trim the excess or make notches at the curved seam allowances. Make a clip on both side gussets where the valley of the "V" shape is; do not cut the thread.

4 **Turn Right side out.** Turn the whole purse piece Right side out through the opening. Use your finger tip or something pointy (but not sharp) to round out the top curved seam.

5 **Press well.** Use an iron to press the purse piece well with a bit of steam to remove the wrinkles if necessary.

6 **Close the opening.** Use Ladder/Blind stitches to close the opening.

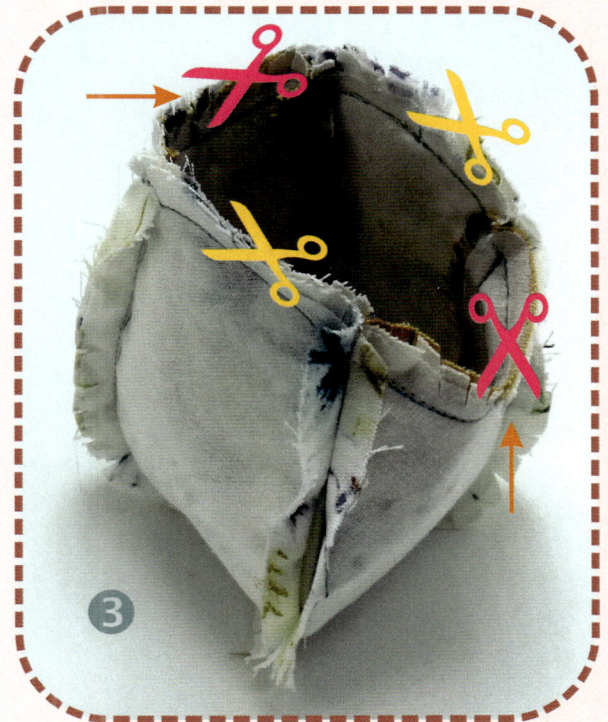

③

This photo was borrowed from the pattern The Katy - "Jade".

⑥

Note

*P*lease refer to the Chapter "Basic Stitches" for more details on how to close the opening.

DIRECTIONS

Complete the Purse piece

7 **Top Stitch.** Top Stitch all the way around the top edge by using 1/16" seam allowance.

✍️ *Do NOT use a seam allowance larger than 1/8", even though the top edge will be under the frame; using a seam allowance smaller than 1/8" will work well.*

8 **Mark all 4 centers.** Press well if needed. Use chalk or erasable pen to mark all 4 centers.

Install the purse frame

1 **Install the purse frame.** Get the correct size and shape purse frame ready to install to the completed purse piece.

✍️ *Please refer to the Chapter "Install Sew-In Purse Frame".*

3.35" Oval

3.35" Oval

EXHIBIT

EXHIBIT

** Please refer to the pattern, "Lauren", for instructions on how to construct this pattern. **

Mila

The Katy - Mila (IV_O_V2)

- **FOUR-piece**
- **Oval Shape Frame**
- **Variation 2**

Finished Size: (approximate measurements)

4" (Top W) x 2.5" (Bottom W)
3.25" (H) x 2.5" (D)

* Top W: the widest part; H: not including the frame;

NOTE:

*The attached pattern has **NO** seam allowances included. Refer to the Chapter "How to Use The Pattern" completely before cutting or sewing!* ☺

Fabric Cuts:

If you are using directional fabric, please make sure they are facing in the right direction.

Tips: *(1) Print 2 copies of the pattern or trace the pattern onto blank paper, (2) add seam allowances to your preference (1/4", 3/8" or 1/2") around one of the patterns, (3) transfer all the markings, (4) cut out the pattern without (Pattern A) and with (Pattern B) seam allowances.*

SEWING SKILL

★ **Beginner/Intermediate**

★★☆☆☆

DIFFICULT LEVEL

★ **Intermediate** ●●●○○

The Katy

Five pieces, *Round* shape frame

Nova

Olivia

Nova

The Katy - Nova (V_R_V1)

- **FIVE-piece**
- **Round Shape Frame**
- **Variation 1**

Finished Size: (approximate measurements)

4.25" (Top W) x 2.5" (Bottom W)
3" (H) x 2.5" (D)

* Top W: the widest part; H: not including the frame;

NOTE:

*The attached pattern has **NO** seam allowances included. Refer to the Chapter "How to Use The Pattern" completely before cutting or sewing! ☺*

Fabric Cuts:

If you are using directional fabric, please make sure they are facing in the right direction.

Tips: *(1) Print 2 copies of the pattern or trace the pattern onto blank paper, (2) add seam allowances to your preference (1/4", 3/8" or 1/2") around one of the patterns, (3) transfer all the markings, (4) cut out the pattern without (Pattern A) and with (Pattern B) seam allowances.*

SEWING SKILL

★ *Beginner/Intermediate*

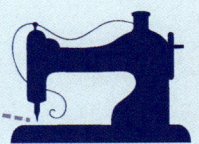

★★☆☆☆

DIFFICULT LEVEL

★ *Intermediate* ●●●○○

PREPARATION

PREPARING ALL THE MATERIALS

✂ For NON-Directional Fabrics

Exterior/Interfacing:

- **Main** fabric - "Front & Back" (Pattern B) x 2; "Side Gusset" (Pattern B) x 2; "Bottom" (Pattern B) x 1;

- **Interfacing** - "Front & Back" (Pattern A) x 2; "Side Gusset" (Pattern A) x 2; "Bottom" (Pattern A) x 1; (no seam allowance needed)

Interior/Interfacing:

- **Lining** fabric - "Front & Back" (Pattern B) x 2; "Side Gusset" (Pattern B) x 2; "Bottom" (Pattern B) x 1;

- **Interfacing** - "Front & Back" (Pattern A) x 2; "Side Gusset" (Pattern A) x 2; "Bottom" (Pattern A) x 1; (no seam allowance needed)

✂ For Directional Fabrics

Exterior/Interfacing:

- **Main** fabric - the same as non-directional fabrics;

- **Interfacing** - the same as above;

Interior/Interfacing:

- **Main** fabric - the same as non-directional fabrics;

- **Interfacing** - the same as above;

Reference

★ For cutting the **Directional fabrics** - please refer to the Chapter *"How to Use The Pattern"*

★ **Pattern A** - the original pattern which has "**NO Seam Allowance**"

★ **Pattern B** - the pattern which has the "**Seam Allowance**" of your choice (1/4", 3/8" or 1/2")

 *P*lease refer to the Section "Apply Interfacing" for more details on how to "Apply Single or Double Layer" interfacing.

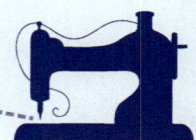

DIRECTIONS

For Directional Fabrics

There is no difference between cutting directional and non-directional fabrics for this 5-piece pattern. If you are using directional fabrics, make sure they are in the correct direction.

Prepare the Materials

1 **Cut the fabrics and interfacing.** You should have 5 pieces of Main/Exterior (2 x "Front & Back", 2 x "Side Gusset" and 1 x "Bottom"), 5 pieces of Lining/Interior (2 x "Front & Back", 2 x "Side Gusset" and 1 x "Bottom") and all the interfacings ready.

2 **Fusing the fabrics.** Apply interfacing to the Wrong side of the main and lining fabrics, following the manufacturer's instructions. Please refer to the Section "Apply Interfacing" for more details.

Lining

1

Single Layer Interfacing

2

Double Layer Interfacing

Main

1

2

Note

*I*f you would like a more structured look, you might want to apply two layers of interfacing. If you would like a softer feel, then a single layer of fleece will work.

DIRECTIONS

Construct the Interior

1 **Trace Pattern A on the Wrong side of the fabrics.** Trace Pattern A (with NO seam allowance) to all the pieces on the Wrong side of the fabric and transfer all the markings as well.

2 **Connect "Front & Back" and "Side Gusset", Align Markings.** Place one of the "Front & Back" pieces, Right side up, under one of the "Side Gusset" pieces, Wrong side up. Align both markings at ① and ②.

✍ *Use pins or clips to hold them in place. Make sure all the markings are aligned.*

3 **Sew.** Sew from ① and stop at ② by using the seam allowance of your choice. Connect all 4 pieces together (2 "Front & Back" pieces,

and 2 "Side Gusset" pieces), connecting "Front & Back" pieces to the "Side Gusset" pieces, alternating between the two until they are all connected (for example: "Front", "Side Gusset", "Back", "Side Gusset", "Front").

DIRECTIONS

Construct the Interior

4 **Connect the "Bottom".** Now, you should have a piece with all 4 sides connected. Let's attach the bottom piece to the Lining piece. The longer sides of the "Bottom" will be attached to the "Front & Back" and the shorter sides of the "Bottom" will be connected to the "Side Gusset".

Make sure all the markings are aligned well, if not, the bottom will look crooked.

5 **Sew all the way around.** Sew all the way around the bottom with the seam allowance of your choice. Start from marking ① and end at marking ②; leave an opening on one of the longer sides.

SLOW DOWN while sewing the corner: Leave the needle down when you reach the corners, lift up the presser foot, pivot the piece, then put the presser foot down and continue sewing.

LEAVE AN OPENING at one of the bottom sides that has the straight seam for turning the whole piece Right side out later.

6 **Make notches and Press well.** Cut notches at all the curved seams. Press all the seam allowances open, trim the excess if necessary. Put aside the completed Lining piece.

Tip

There are two other ways to sew the Lining piece.
 1). Connect the "Bottom" piece to the two "Front & Back" pieces first. Then connect the "Side Gusset" pieces.
2). Connect the "Bottom" to the "Side Gusset" pieces first. Then connect the "Front & Back" pieces.
Do not forget to LEAVE AN OPENING.

DIRECTIONS

Construct the Exterior

1 **Construct the exterior** using the same process as you did with the lining, except you do NOT need to leave an opening. Sew the exterior by using the seam allowance of your choice.

*NO need to leave an opening. **SEW SLOWLY** on the bottom, right-angle corners and all the curved seams.*

Complete the Purse piece

1 **Get both Main and Lining pieces ready to connect.** You should have both Main and Lining pieces ready to complete the purse piece. Place the Main piece (Right side out) into the Lining piece (Wrong side out), with the Right sides of both pieces facing each other. Align all 4 center markings.

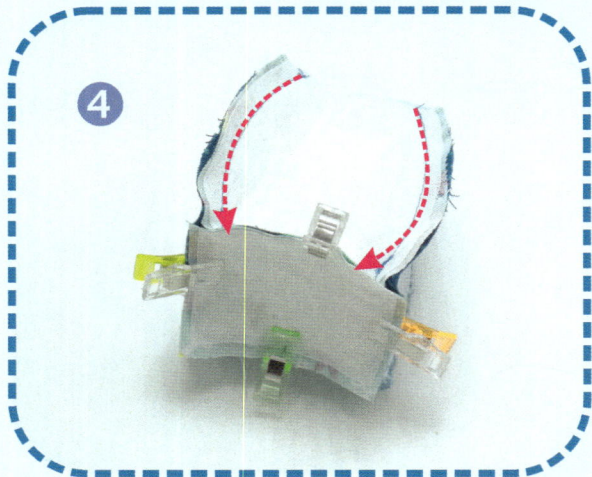

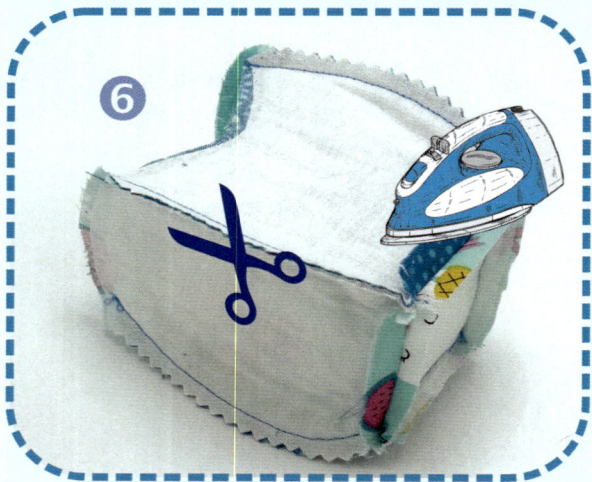

*Use chalk or erasable pen to draw the seam line on the Wrong side of the Lining **before** sewing.*

DIRECTIONS

Complete the Purse piece

2 **Sew all the way around.** Sew all the way around the top edge to connect both pieces with the seam allowance of your choice.

3 **Trim.** Use Pinking Shears to trim the excess or make notches at the curved seam allowances. Make a clip on both side gussets where the valley of the "V" shape is; do not cut the thread.

4 **Turn Right side out.** Turn the whole purse piece Right side out through the opening. Use your finger tip or something pointy (but not sharp) to round out the top curved seam.

5 **Press well.** Use an iron to press the purse piece well with a bit of steam to remove the wrinkles if necessary.

6 **Close the opening.** Use Ladder/Blind stitches to close the opening.

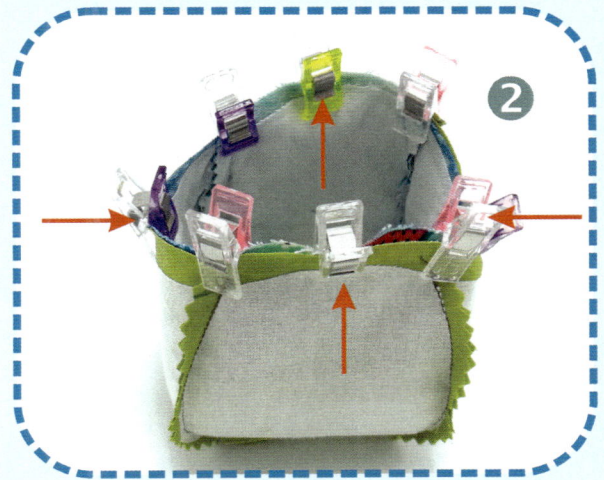

DIRECTIONS

Complete the Purse piece

7 **Top Stitch.** Top Stitch all the way around the top edge by using 1/16" seam allowance.

✎ *Do NOT use a seam allowance larger than 1/8", even though the top edge will be under the frame; using a seam allowance smaller than 1/8" will work well.*

8 **Mark all 4 centers.** Press well if needed. Use chalk or erasable pen to mark all 4 centers.

Install the purse frame

1 **Install the purse frame.** Get the correct size and shape purse frame ready to install to the completed purse piece.

✎ *Please refer to the Chapter "Install Sew-In Purse Frame".*

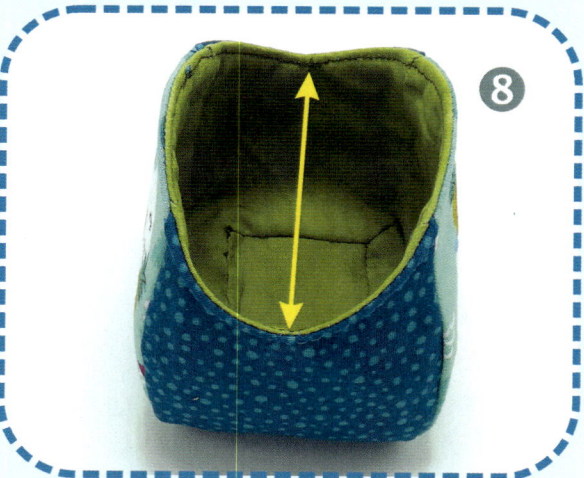

3.35" Round

The Katy - *Nova*

3.35" (8.5 cm) Arch Purse Frame

V_R_V1

Front & Back

No Seam Allowance

The Katy - *Olivia*

3.35" (8.5 cm) Arch Purse Frame

V_R_V2

Front & Back

No Seam Allowance

The Katy - *Nova*

3.35" (8.5 cm) Arch Purse Frame

V_R_V1

Side Gusset

No Seam Allowance

The Katy - *Olivia*

3.35" (8.5 cm) Arch Purse Frame

V_R_V2

Side Gusset

No Seam Allowance

The Katy - *Nova*

V_R_V1

Bottom

No Seam Allowance

1"

The Katy - *Olivia*

V_R_V2

Bottom

No Seam Allowance

** Please refer to the pattern, "Nova", for instructions on how to construct this pattern. **

Olivia

The Katy - Olivia (V_R_V2)

- **FIVE-piece**
- **Round Shape Frame**
- **Variation 2**

Finished Size: (approximate measurements)

4.5" (Top W) x 2.75" (Bottom W)
3.5" (H) x 2.5" (D)

* Top W: the widest part; H: not including the frame;

> **NOTE:**
>
> *The attached pattern has __NO__ seam allowances included. Refer to the Chapter "How to Use The Pattern" completely before cutting or sewing!* ☺

Fabric Cuts:

If you are using directional fabric, please make sure they are facing in the right direction.

Tips: *(1) Print 2 copies of the pattern or trace the pattern onto blank paper, (2) add seam allowances to your preference (1/4", 3/8" or 1/2") around one of the patterns, (3) transfer all the markings, (4) cut out the pattern without (Pattern A) and with (Pattern B) seam allowances.*

This photo was borrowed from the pattern The Katy - "Nova".

SEWING SKILL

★ *Beginner/Intermediate*

★★☆☆☆

DIFFICULT LEVEL

★ *Intermediate* ●●●○○

EXHIBIT

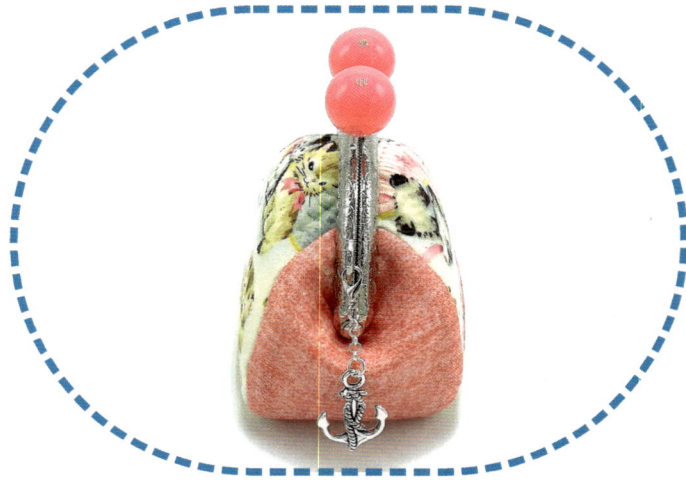

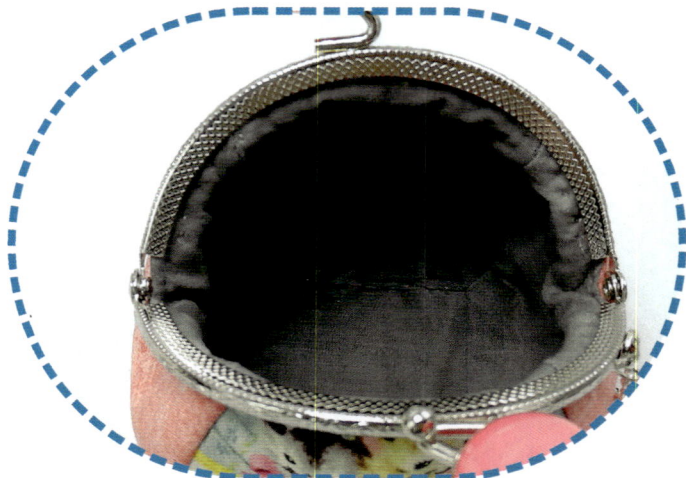

About the Author
Jacine Wang

*A*fter graduating from graduate school, having majored in Computer Science, she became a stay-at-home mom for the past twenty-five years. Before her youngest son went to college two years ago, she began wondering what she would do when the house became an "empty nest". As a result, the whole family decided to adopt two adorable kittens to be her companions at home. The two kittens solved the issue of being lonely, but this didn't resolve the transition going from being a busy mother, taking care of the kids and housework, to having little to nothing to do every day. Incidentally, she wanted to make a hammock for her two cute kitties which requires a little bit sewing. She didn't like sewing at all, because she would always poke herself with the needle by accident. This led her to think about using a sewing machine instead. People who know how to use a sewing machine don't think it is difficult to use, but she knew nothing about operating a sewing machine, at all. She is a self-learner starting from scratch and now enjoys designing handbag patterns and sewing as well. While she is sewing, her two pretty kitties, Asti and Celine, are on or under her sewing table, napping or playing, sometimes lying on the fabrics to get her attention while she works. If she, who knew nothing about sewing, can sew, "sew" can you.

Jacine lives in Plano, Texas with her husband, Charles, and they have two kids, Christine and Johnathan, who are working towards a music degree.

Project Index

Pattern Index:
Ava ....51~52
Brooklyn ....52~53
Charlotte....57~58
Daisy..........58~59
Evelyn ....73~74
Faith 85
Grace................87
Hope................100
Iris 101

The Katy - I_O

Brooklyn   Ava

The Katy - I_R

Evelyn   Daisy

Charlotte

41

56

The Katy - II_R

Faith

The Katy - III_R

Grace

Hope   Iris

The Katy - IV_R

Jade

Kaylee

75

The Katy - IV_O

86

The Katy - V_R

112

Pattern Index:
Jade..................113
Kaylee 113
Lauren 127
Mila 127
Nova................149
Olivia 149

Mila

Lauren

Olivia

Nova

126

139